TREE WISDOM

TREE WISDOM

A JOURNEY OF WISDOM, SYMBOLS, HEALING, AND RENEWAL

Alice Peck

Illustrations by **Melissa Launay**

CICO BOOKS

LONDON NEW YORK

*As always, this book is for Duane
and Tyl with so much love—you are
my roots and samaras.*

This edition published in 2023 by CICO Books
An imprint of Ryland Peters & Small Ltd
20–21 Jockey's Fields   341 E 116th St
London WC1R 4BW   New York, NY 10029

www.rylandpeters.com

10 9 8 7 6 5 4 3 2 1

First published in 2016 as *Be More Tree*

A CIP catalog record for this book is available from the
Library of Congress and the British Library.

ISBN: 978-1-80065-263-7

Printed in China

Editor: Helen Ridge   Art director: Sally Powell
Senior designer: Emily Breen   Creative director: Leslie Harrington
Illustrator: Melissa Launay   Head of production: Patricia Harrington
                                  Publishing manager: Penny Craig
                                  Publisher: Cindy Richards

Disclaimer
The information in this book including but not limited to text and
images is for informational purposes only. It is not intended to be a
substitute for professional medical advice, diagnosis, or treatment.
The reader should regularly consult a physician in matters relating
to his/her health and particularly with respect to any symptoms
that may require diagnosis or medical attention.

Note
Every effort has been made to contact and acknowledge copyright
holders of all material included in this book. The publisher and
author apologize for any errors or omissions that may remain and
ask that these omissions be brought to their attention so that they
may be corrected in further editions.

CONTENTS

INTRODUCTION

I leaned against a large rock, still warm from the day, and lost myself in the companionship of trees.

From *A Thousand Voices* (2010) by Jeri Parker

I live in an area of Brooklyn called Red Hook. It's a mixed residential and industrial neighborhood on New York Harbor. I love Red Hook because it feels to me like a combination of the two places where I grew up: Detroit and Cape Cod. Behind our tiny house flourishes a huge maple tree, which has been beautifully portrayed on the right. I'm not a botanist, but our house is about a century old and I believe the tree is a bit older. Its foliage fills the view from our back windows in spring, summer, and autumn. In winter, its branches outline the sunrise. The maple lives in proximity to us but follows a different, mightier schedule. Its presence keeps my family's city life connected to nature, to something bigger than the stuff of our day-to-day.

In 2012, when Hurricane Sandy struck the East Coast of the United States, Red Hook was labeled "Zone A" and evacuated. My husband, son, and I sandbagged our house, wrangled our dogs and cats, and went to stay with friends on higher ground. As we watched the news reports of the storm surging through our community, I kept wondering about "our" tree. Would it survive?

We returned to a devastated landscape. Floodwater isn't pretty or pure and the cleanup took months. Many neighbors lost all they had: every child's drawing, every pillowcase, and every book. We were lucky—our ground floor had only a thin layer of muck left behind after the water receded. Seawater corroded our old boiler, but that was the worst of the damage. Best of all, the old maple, which had weathered hurricanes even before they had names like Hazel and Flossy and Bob, made it through Sandy. Some branches had cracked and fallen, but the trunk stood rooted strong. I was so grateful the maple endured that I began taking photographs of it from our window as part of my morning meditation. I posted one of my Red Hook Tree photos on Facebook. I did it again. And again… Suddenly, the tree had fans.

Contemplating my tree was always bigger than the photos and the "likes" for me. The more I looked at the maple, the more my observation of its intricacies and changes became a way to connect to my world and myself. There are many ways to meditate and be with trees: just by sitting near one, or through ancient wisdom practices, poetry, science, history, and healing. Trees are ubiquitous—almost everybody has access to one. They tell a complete and ongoing story—from their deep taproots to the birds that alight on their delicate high branches. Trees reflect our lives through their perseverance and seasonal rhythms—always changing yet constant. They evolve along a much more protracted timetable than humans. My maple is no exception. This realization led me to think about how we can learn from "tree wisdom" and *be more tree*…

As I looked for answers to these questions, I became inspired by so many great writers, observers, and poets, from Henry David Thoreau to David George Haskell, Edward Abbey to Anna Botsford Comstock, John Muir to Stephanie Kaza. I loved how they each took a place—for example, Thoreau's Walden and Haskell's one square meter of old growth forest in Tennessee—and looked, truly looked, at the trees, and then looked some more. They put into practice the philosopher Martin Heidegger's "being-in-the-world" and went beyond subject and object, self

and nature. The images by the photographer Thomas Pakenham in his *Meetings with Remarkable Trees* series (1996) do this, as do the canny, charming, and wise descriptions by the author Hugh Johnson in *The World of Trees* (2010), and the musings of numerous other writers, artists, and scientists that you'll find in this book and its bibliography. "These trees shall be my books…" wrote William Shakespeare in *As You Like It*. For me, the reverse holds true as well: these books shall be my trees. I don't live in the woods, but I took what I could from my little backyard, my maple through the seasons, my bookshelves, the local library—*my* woods—and that's what you have in this book. It is something between a commonplace book and a miscellany seeded in a love of trees. This book is my subjective and, hopefully, artful collection of some of the ways trees, grounded and soaring, steady and move me—and, I hope, you as well.

I've divided this book into four sections: Roots, Branches, Leaves, and Seeds. Roots presents the ways we can better understand our world by paying attention to trees—how their histories guide us. Branches considers the symbolism of trees and how their lore is woven into our lives. Leaves is more practical, containing (mostly) tangible ways that trees can heal us and the world. Finally, Seeds is about the spirit of trees, how they transform us both physically and spiritually, and how important it is that we protect them so that they can continue to do so for generations to come. Each entry includes an application, a meditation, a prayer, or a mantra—something readers can do to be more tree.

As you read, you'll see that these four sections are useful but arbitrary. The book could have been organized in many different ways; by the Latin or common names of the trees, geography, or leaf form. I hope you'll start with one of the sections, then veer off the path meandering between the trunks and the saplings—let olive take you to pear, or birch to sequoia. As in a forest, the joy and the discovery are in the wandering.

PART I
ROOTS

Wisdom, Lore, and Understanding 12

Wisdom, Lore, and Understanding

No matter what their species, trees have roots—they are their source, their foundation, and their means of sustenance. Roots depend upon three things: oxygen, water, and space to grow. As they seek nourishment to send to their branches, some tree roots travel horizontally, others downward into the soil. The distance for some is so shallow that it can be measured in inches, while others penetrate as deep as two hundred feet.

Like trees, we humans are anchored and nourished by our roots—familial and cultural—and depend upon what's unseen—myths, symbols, and meaning—to help us make sense of our lives. Trees provide an abundance of examples as they illuminate our conscious and subconscious selves, our histories, and even our archetypes.

Consider the vast, 80,000-year-old colony of quaking aspens called the Pando in Fishlake National Forest in Utah. The 40,000 trees are connected by a single root system. The roots remain constant even as the aspen is constantly sending out fresh growth. Thinking about the Pando's roots and shoots—the newborn intrinsically entwined with the ancient—can put our world and the interconnection of all beings into perspective in one way. The erudition of the psychologist Carl Jung gives us another. He saw the oak tree as a prototype for the psyche, or self, and its roots as a metaphor for the unconscious. The aspen and the oak are just the beginning.

Exploring the trees in this section of the book helps us to consider how we are rooted in time, like the cedar that connects us to ancient Mesopotamia and yet is as present as the pencil in our hand, like the chestnut trees featured in so many great books and poems, or like the story of cinnamon that contains a history of the modern world. Trees are the source of both beauty and darkness, as the ephemeral cherry blossom and the complexity of the yew show us. Roots are the beginnings of the mysteries of the juniper, the wisdom of the kauri, and the secrets of the laurel and rowan.

When it comes to roots, I've learned so much about patience and presence, not just from the ailanthus, mango, and steady oak, but also from the tree in my backyard. The root systems of maples are typically dense and overwhelming, forcing out the growth of other vegetation. Mine is no exception. Being a city tree, its challenges go beyond drought or winter freeze and include pavement obstacles and shadows cast by buildings. Yet, the maple perseveres, and so for me teaches both the wisdom and folly of tenacity.

In all great arts, as in trees, it is the height that charms us; we care nothing for the roots or trunks, yet it could not be without the aid of these.

Marcus Tullius Cicero, Roman philosopher, 107–43 BCE

Chestnut

The chestnut is beloved all over the world. In Victorian England, the Sunday before Ascension Day was named Chestnut Sunday, and Londoners visited Kew Gardens to celebrate the newly emerging chestnut blossoms. Part of the traditional New Year's menu in Japan, chestnuts symbolize both success and strife, mastery and strength. The tree has been cultivated in Asia since before rice, perhaps for as long as 6,000 years. It might also be the most literary of trees. It features prominently in George Orwell's *1984* and novels by writers from Honoré de Balzac to E. M. Forster, Charlotte Brontë to Ray Bradbury. Poets, too, including Yeats, Basho, and Longfellow, have celebrated it.

The nineteenth-century Sicilian poet Giuseppe Borrello wrote of the Hundred Horse Chestnut on the eastern slope of Mount Etna: "A chestnut tree/ was so large/ that its branches formed an umbrella/ under which refuge was sought from the rain/ from thunder bolts and flashes of lightning…" (Translator unknown.) According to legend, the tree was given its name after a queen of Aragon and her company of one hundred knights were caught in a brutal storm and took shelter under its boughs. Until recently, the tree that inspired Borrello was the largest and longest-lived chestnut in the world. It was an old tree when Plato was alive! Believed to have lived for millennia—between two and four thousand years—it was the largest tree ever recorded, measuring 190 feet

---

In June the chestnut shot its blossomed spires
Of silver upward 'mid the foliage dark
As if some sylvan deity had hung
Its dim umbrageousness with votive wreaths.

David Macbeth Moir, Scottish physician and writer
(1798–1851)

APPRECIATE WHAT YOU HAVE

The chestnut tree's wisdom is in reminding us of the impermanence of seemingly permanent things. Take a moment to pause and think about the chestnut— so enduring and powerful, yet fragile. Apply those thoughts to all in our lives we take for granted, who we assume will always be there, and then pause to appreciate what we have.

---

in circumference in 1780, and grew to be over 1,200 meters tall. The legend of the Hundred Horse Chestnut has lived for centuries and so have its roots, but not all parts of the tree are quite so old—parts of the trunk have been burned, and its branches used for firewood. According to an issue of *The Garden* from December 1888, "It is said that a shepherd's house is built in the hollow of the trunk, and during the winter the waste wood supplies him with sufficient fuel while the nuts furnish him with abundance of food through the latter part of the summer." That shepherd is long gone, but the stories and tree live on, still a favorite of travellers.

As enduring as the chestnut tree is, the lesson it offers is one of the transitory nature of things, and of life. We tend to see blossoms, like those of the cherry, as icons of fleeting reality, but the ancient chestnut represents impermanence in its own way. At the start of the nineteenth century, it was one of the primary trees in the eastern American woodlands but, in 1906, a bark fungus similar to Dutch elm disease took hold and killed over *three billion* trees. By 1940, chestnuts became rare throughout the United States. As a result, the American Chestnut Cooperators' Foundation was formed to reforest with chestnut trees, but its work will take decades.

Laurel

In *The Metamorphoses*, the Roman poet Ovid presents his version of the ancient Greek myth of the goddess Athena transforming the river nymph Daphne into the original laurel tree so that she can escape Apollo's amorous pursuit. Her arms were turned into branches, her hair into leaves, and her feet into roots. Only her beauty remained. The laurel became sacred to Apollo, and was used to crown the victors at the Pythian Games—a forerunner of the modern Olympic Games—held in Delphi in his honor. Since then, the tree has been used to represent victory in the Western world.

In ancient Greek, the word for laurel is *daphne*. *The Homeric Hymns*, a collection of poems written in the seventh century BCE, tells of the oracles of Delphi, the priestesses who spoke for Apollo. The laurel has historically been associated with their rituals; the first oracle at Delphi was called "Laurel," and ancient texts recount these seers chewing laurel leaves to induce trances and visions. Prophesy may not be our first thought when adding a few bay laurel leaves to a soup or a tomato sauce, but the ancient Greeks used them as seasoning as cooks do today, to give a mild floral fragrance to food.

From Greek lore came laurel wreaths, looking to your laurels, resting on your laurels, studying for the baccalaureate, and poet laureates. During the Renaissance, laurel imagery was emblematic of poetic inspiration. Because of this and the poetry in the paired names of the two types of laurel tree—the mountain and the bay—I like to think of the laurel as the poets' tree. It inspired not only Louisa May Alcott and Ovid, but also Lord Byron and William Blake, Dante and Emily Dickinson, Goethe and Allen Ginsberg, William Herrick and Horace, Andrew Marvell and Edna St. Vincent Millay, John Skelton and Shelley, and many more.

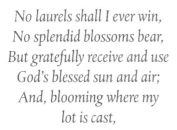

No laurels shall I ever win,
No splendid blossoms bear,
But gratefully receive and use
God's blessed sun and air;
And, blooming where my
lot is cast,
Grow happy and content,
Making some barren spot
more fair,
For a humble life well spent.

From *A Garland for Girls* by Louisa May Alcott, novelist (1832–1888)

INSPIRED BY LAURELS

Laurel leaves are the stuff of victory, supper, and poetic inspiration. Try giving something back to the laurel tree by writing a poem. It doesn't have to be fancy or formal, it doesn't even have to be on paper—just some phrases of gratitude to honor all that the laurel represents. What does the laurel mean to you?

Ailanthus

Some people call the ailanthus the ghetto palm, stink tree, urban weed, or tree of hell. The Chinese name for it, *chòuchūn*, translates as "foul-smelling tree." But others call it the tree of heaven or urban lotus. Whether beloved or reviled, the ailanthus teaches us tenacity and balance. In her novel *A Tree Grows in Brooklyn*, Betty Smith made the ailanthus a symbol of aspiration and overcoming adversity.

Native to Asia, the ailanthus was imported to England from China in the eighteenth century, and from there it spread all over the West. It's considered an invasive species and can force out native trees. Opportunistic and fast-growing, even amid garbage or through concrete, ailanthus can reach up to fifty feet in twenty-five years. It is persistent, but doesn't live long compared to most trees: only about fifty years. It's surculose, which means that it produces suckers (root sprouts) that grow from buds at the base, and new trees can sprout even if the trunks have been cut down.

In 1985, when the artist Isamu Noguchi was breaking ground for the museum named for him in Long Island City, New York, he discovered a sixty-foot-tall ailanthus tree on the site, flourishing exactly in the center of his planned sculpture garden. Noguchi did a remarkable thing—he didn't have the tree chopped down, but rather built the garden around it. In 2008, the seventy-five-year-old tree was dying and had to be removed, but its story didn't end there. The museum contacted the Detroit Tree of Heaven Woodshop, an artists' collective that works primarily with ailanthus, to carve and construct furniture from the old tree that is now used in the museum.

"The ailanthus is well known for regenerating from its roots," the Noguchi Museum's director, Jenny Dixon, told *The New York Times*. "If it revives, the original could be here again, as a symbol for the museum."

PRACTICING PATIENCE

The ailanthus can teach us about balance and determination. Considering this tree, which is loved as well as reviled, can be a way to practice what the Zen Buddhists might call "just enough" as we remember that if we're patient and persistent, wonderful things take root in unexpected ways.

Ailanthus… was known as… Tree of Heaven, from its rapid growth toward the sky.

Meehans' Monthly: A Magazine of Horticulture, Botany, and Kindred Subjects, 1894

Aspen

As a child, I was fascinated by aspen trees and how animated their leaves appeared. In summer, I would look to them to gauge the weather, since I knew the saying, "When leaves show their undersides, be very sure rain betides." You will appreciate the truth in this if you observe aspen leaves fluttering as they react to the increase in humidity preceding a storm. There is so much motion because their petioles, the leafstalks that join the leaves, are long and flattened and tremble, or quake, in the slightest breeze. This is why we think of aspens as whispering, tremulous, and even magical.

Now that I'm older, I'm more intrigued that a tree can represent communication, and for me the aspen helps to put life into perspective and demonstrates how to acknowledge the interconnection of all beings. Like the ailanthus, aspens are surculose, having long root suckers that travel laterally, some as far as twenty-six feet from the original tree trunk. They grow in clonal—genetically identical—colonies, derived from a single seedling. Some of these root colonies live for *thousands* of years, perhaps as long as 80,000 years. One of the oldest living colonies of quaking aspens is the Pando (which means "I spread" in Latin) in Fishlake National Forest, Utah. Nicknamed the "Trembling Giant," these 105 acres of aspens are connected by a single root system. The trees die off but new shoots continue to spring up. Aspens even survive forest fires because, although the leaves, branches, and trunks above ground may be burned, the tenacious roots endure, sending up new shoots in the spring. There is poetry to a colony of trees being one of the oldest living organisms on Earth yet still producing new growth at this very moment.

When we try to pick out anything by itself, we find it hitched to everything else in the universe. One fancies a heart like our own must be beating in every crystal and cell, and we feel like stopping to speak to the plants and animals as fellow friendly mountaineers.

From *My First Summer in the Sierra* by John Muir, naturalist (1838–1914)

"ONLY CONNECT!"

The aspen gives us an opportunity to acknowledge our interdependence with everything on the planet. Like the clonal aspen, all human community is interconnected. We can meditate on the aspen to acknowledge what we can let go of in our lives and what we can allow to sprout and bloom to nourish and provide fresh paths of relationship. As E.M. Forster wrote in *Howards End*, "Only connect!"

Juniper

Some trees are more magical than others... and the smoke of the juniper has a tremendous amount of sacred lore associated with it. As long ago as 430 BCE, the Greek physician Hippocrates said that the smoke from burning its berries could be used as a fumigant and to treat the plague. In Scotland and Ireland, it was traditional to sain (consecrate, protect, or bless a space) with juniper smoke. Throughout Central Europe, juniper was burned in fires in the days leading up to Beltane (May Day) or the spring equinox, to drive away demons and bless a household and its inhabitants. The lore of the Native American Hopis tells of how the Earth's caretaking spirit traveled with the juniper tree, and so they traditionally used juniper smoke to make a space sacred, while the Native American Cree used it to treat asthma. In Italy, juniper was added to fires so that the smoke would ward off the evil eye. From the Arctic to tropical Africa to the mountains of Central America, it has been believed that burning incense from the juniper tree actively connects to the sacred.

In the Himalayan regions and among Tibetan Buddhists worldwide, juniper smoke is deemed sacred and is a primary ingredient of incense. Burning it is part of an ancient ritual called *zampling ji sang*. It is believed that the juniper is the abode of the goddesses of fertility and good fortune. Lamas burn the sacred wood, and the fragrant smoke wafting from most Tibetan temples and shrines purifies all it reaches.

In northern Mongolia, near the Russian border, shamans, called *boos*, are still practicing today, and there is an increasing number taking up their tradition since the end of the Soviet era. These shamans act as an intermediary between humans and the spirit world, and they use juniper smoke to attract spirits. When chanting, dancing, and praying to achieve an ecstatic trance, they burn juniper twigs; the smoke is said to please the spirits and summon them to Earth.

Similarly, the shamans, or *bitans*, of the Hanzakut people in the Karkoram Mountains of Pakistan practice a juniper rite to connect to supernatural beings. They burn juniper bushes, inhale the smoke, drink blood from a goat's head, and dance to ecstatic music. Their resulting trance is believed to be the result of the hallucinogenic elements in juniper smoke, and their actions serve to connect them to the Divine.

GLIMPSING THE COSMIC DANCE

Using juniper smoke, we too can find the mystical in the ordinary—no goat's head required! The next time you're at a campfire or fireside, add some fallen juniper branches. Inhale the fragrance and consider the smoke and how it can represent a physical connection to the unknown.

When we are alone on a starlit night, when by chance we see the migrating birds in autumn descending on a grove of junipers to rest and eat ... ; at such times the awakening, the turning inside out of all values, the "newness," the emptiness and the purity of vision that make themselves evident, all these provide a glimpse of the cosmic dance.

From *New Seeds of Contemplation* by Thomas Merton, writer and mystic (1915–1968)

Cherry

Live in simple faith…
Just as this trusting cherry
Flowers, fades, and falls

Haiku by Kobayashi Issa (1763–1828),
translated by Peter Beilenson

Growing up in Michigan, I was taught that Traverse City was the "Cherry Capital of the World." Although the denizens have secured a place in Guinness World Records for baking the world's largest cherry pie (over seventeen feet in diameter and weighing 28,350 pounds), it turns out that Turkey is actually the largest producer of cultivated cherries, followed by the United States, then Iran.

Cherries inspire celebration, and cherry festivals are held all over the world. In March, *Fiesta del Cerezo en Flor* honors the blossoming of over two million cherry trees in Spain's Jerte Valley. Cherry Blossom Day is observed in April in Sweden. The Brooklyn Botanic Garden, New York, which has the most diverse flowering cherry collection outside of Japan, holds a Sakura Matsuri street festival every spring. There are more events elsewhere, from Canada to Brazil to Denmark, but Japan is where it all started.

It is no wonder the cherry flower is considered a symbol of Japan. The eighth-century *Nihon shoki*, the second oldest book of classical Japanese history, recounts *hanami*, or flower-viewing parties, held as early as the third century. The Feast of the Sight of the Cherry Blossoms, or *sakura*, became a favorite practice of the Imperial Court in Japan during the Heian Period (794–1185), but it is now celebrated all over the country. Every year, the Japan Weather Association tracks the moment of the peak cherry bloom, and when the trees flower, families gather to picnic under the trees.

Why celebrate the cherry when there are so many other trees with astonishing blossom? Perhaps it is because of the intensity of their bloom and the speed with which they fall. Perhaps it is because they are akin to fragrant clouds, and so have become a symbol of purity and beauty. The Japanese see the blooming as representing the passage of time, transience, impermanence, and mortality. There is a term in Japanese aesthetics, *mono no aware*, which means "the pathos of things," and the cherry blossom—which is so very vital and beautiful, and then fallen and gone—is frequently associated with it. I find it particularly moving that cherry blossoms were used to represent samurai warriors—"they who do not fear death"—and that during World War II kamikaze pilots painted cherry blossoms on their planes before leaving on their fatal missions.

Mango

The mango is one of my son's favorite fruits, although probably not because of the mango cultivar 'Alice' that originated in Florida and shares its name with mine. Interestingly, there is a mango for almost every letter of the alphabet: Banganapalli, Cogshall, Dasheri, Emerald, Fajri Kalan, Gary, Himsagar, Ice Cream, Jakarta, Kalepad, Langra, Mallika, Neelam, Osteen, Parvin, Ruby, Sindhri, Totapuri, Van Dyke, Young, and Zill.

The mango tree is writ large in Buddhist lore. Buddha is said to have meditated with his followers in mango groves, and received the gift of one near the ancient Indian city of Vaisali from the courtesan Amrapali, his patron and convert. King Tissa, who reigned in the nation now known as Sri Lanka from 307 to 267 BCE, supposedly converted to Buddhism under a mango tree. Because of the legend of the Buddha causing a complete mango tree to sprout from the seed moments after eating the fruit, the tree is considered

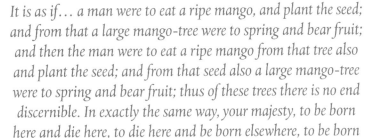

holy. In Sanskrit poetry, mangos are also referred to as *kalpavriksha*—wish-granting trees.

In Hinduism, the perfectly ripe mango is often held by the elephant god Ganesh as a symbol of spiritual fruition or attainment, encouraging everyone to see his or her potential for perfection. The tree is sacred to the Hindu god Shiva and his consort Parvati, and there is a 3,500-year-old mango tree at Ekambareswarar Temple, dedicated to Shiva, in Kanchipuram, India, that has branches said to yield four different types of mango. The great nineteenth-century Urdu poet Mirza Asadullah Khan (or Ghalib) wrote of his love of mangos, and Rabindranath Tagore, the Bengali Renaissance man and first non-European to win the Nobel Prize in Literature, wrote odes to their blossoms.

MINDFUL FRUIT

The mango's wisdom reminds us of the music and mystery of the cycles of life. It may be hard to find a mango tree, but it is far easier to procure a mango fruit. Savor it as a practice of mindfulness, one slow, sweet bite at a time. When you reach the seed, think of the tree it was and the tree it could become again.

It is as if… a man were to eat a ripe mango, and plant the seed; and from that a large mango-tree were to spring and bear fruit; and then the man were to eat a ripe mango from that tree also and plant the seed; and from that seed also a large mango-tree were to spring and bear fruit; thus of these trees there is no end discernible. In exactly the same way, your majesty, to be born here and die here, to die here and be born elsewhere, to be born there and die there, to die there and be born elsewhere, this, your majesty, is the round of existence.

From the Buddhist text *Milinda Pañha* (c.100 BCE), translated by Henry Clarke Warren

Kauri

Native to New Zealand, Australia, and the Philippines, kauris are huge coniferous trees that grow straight upward. Although New Zealand is about 9,000 miles from my home in Brooklyn, the wisdom of the kauri is nevertheless profound for me. These trees can teach us to take responsibility for our actions.

When the Māori arrived in New Zealand from Polynesia in the late thirteenth century, the kauri tree was already there. In his *Voyage of the Beagle* (1839), Charles Darwin remarked on its nobility: "These trees are remarkable for their smooth cylindrical boles, which run up to a height of sixty, and even ninety feet, with a nearly equal diameter, and without a single branch. The crown of branches at the summit is out of all proportion small to the trunk; and the leaves are likewise small compared with the branches." He also recognized the value of its timber, as had Captain Cook when he arrived in New Zealand a century earlier and first saw a kauri forest.

Like so many other indigenous trees, the kauri has been over-logged. They're also dying from a soil-spread fungus called "dieback disease," which has led to conservationists enforcing sanctions and building platforms to protect the trees' roots. Nevertheless, many magnificent kauri remain. The most iconic is Tane Mahuta, in Waipoua Forest, believed to be the tallest on the planet—over fifty-eight feet high with a girth of over forty-five feet. It is estimated to be 2,000 years old. The tree's name honors Tane, the Māori god of the forest, who was the child of the sky god and the earth goddess. Tane grew between his parents to bring light, so that everything between them—the natural world—could proliferate and thrive. It is believed that all the trees in the forest play their part in holding up the sky.

The Māori see all living creatures as Tane Mahuta's children, and believe that everything in nature possesses a spirit. The tree is no different. When humans have to slay (chop down) one of their kauri relatives to build canoes or houses, solemn rituals and prayers called *karakia* are performed, asking forgiveness of the trees for taking their *mauri*, or life force, from the forest.

Ki te kore nga putake e mākukungia e kore te rakau e tupu.
(If the roots of the tree are not watered, the tree will never grow.)

Māori proverb

Cinnamon

The spice we call cinnamon comes from the inner bark of several trees of the *Cinnamomum* genus, including "true cinnamon" and cassia. Although it is native to Bangladesh, Sri Lanka, India, and Burma, cinnamon has been treasured around the Mediterranean and across the Middle East since antiquity. Spice traders protected their sources, and during medieval times, misinformation—such as crusaders reporting that cinnamon was fished from the River Nile in nets—fostered the mystery of the spice's origins.

The Greek historian Herodotus, who lived in the fifth century BCE, added to the confusion by writing of giant cinnamon birds. According to him, the birds collected sticks from a mysterious country where cinnamon trees grew, and used them to build their nests on high cliffs throughout Arabia. Resourceful harvesters would chop up animal carcasses and leave them for the birds to find. They flew down, gathered the chunks of meat, and took them back to their nests. The added weight caused the nests to break from the cliffs and fall to the ground, making the cinnamon easy to gather.

The cinnamon tree continued to play a complex role in history. From the thirteenth century, Indonesian traders transported the spice to East Africa, where it was sold and taken north. Italy held a monopoly on its trade, distributing the spice in Europe until the Mamluks and Ottomans took over their routes, leading Europeans to search for alternative sources. In the early sixteenth century, Portuguese traders arrived on "the cinnamon isle" of Ceylon—now Sri Lanka—built up cinnamon production, erected a fort, and had their own monopoly for a century. Dutch traders then took over, expelling the Portuguese by 1658, and began cultivating their own trees. A century later, the British gained control of Ceylon, but over time the cinnamon trade there declined as the trees were grown in other countries, and the production of coffee, sugar, and tea replaced it.

LINKING TO HISTORY

The cinnamon tree reminds us that every object has a history that becomes a part of us when we interact with it. Everything has a story behind it, and everything we touch has passed through other hands. With the understanding of cinnamon lore comes a reminder to think of all the people involved throughout the history of humanity that led to that sprinkle of the spice on our toast or in a cookie.

The shores of the island are full of it… and it is the best in all the Orient. When one is downwind of the island, one can still smell cinnamon eight leagues out to sea.

From a letter written by a seventeenth-century Dutch sea captain

Hawthorn

Throughout the Western world, the hawthorn is traditionally seen as an evil tree. French peasants believed it was the source of Jesus's crown of thorns and that the trees wept, sighed, and groaned every year on Good Friday, the day of Christ's crucifixion. Other traditions say that hawthorns scream when chopped, that it's dangerous to sleep under them because fairies dance there at night, that banshees live in them, and that witches make their brooms from the branches. It was a long-held superstition that to build a house from hawthorn meant you wouldn't live long.

As recently as 1982, chopping down a hawthorn was believed to have dire consequences. When the American automaker John Delorean built his factory outside Belfast, Northern Ireland, to manufacture his eponymous cars, he wanted to remove a hawthorn that grew on the property. Despite protestations from his superstitious workers, he is said to have taken it upon himself to bulldoze the tree. Four years later, Delorean's company was in financial ruin and he was arrested on cocaine trafficking charges.

> *By the craggy hillside,*
> *Through the mosses bare,*
> *They have planted thorn-trees*
> *For pleasure here and there.*
>
> *Is any man so daring*
> *As dig them up in spite,*
> *He shall find their sharpest thorns*
> *In his bed at night.*

From *The Fairies* by William Allingham (1824–1889)

GOOD AND BAD

What can heal a heart can also stop a heart. Where there is good, there is evil, and the hawthorn is more of an unresolved contradiction than a display of harmonious balance. Considering its dual nature, we can look for the best in things while remaining conscious of the dangers that may lie within.

In spring, when the hawthorn blooms, the lore shifts from gloom to hope and love. Throughout Europe, it was believed that tying ribbons among the leaves would grant wishes. In France, twigs were put in cradles for protection. The ancient Greeks carried branches in wedding processions and used them to decorate the altar of Hymenaeus, the god of marriage ceremonies. Irish superstition may have deemed the tree unlucky, but it also empowered the hawthorn with healing a broken heart.

These healing powers aren't just legendary. Hawthorn has historically been a reliable herbal medicine, used by Native Americans and Europeans to treat heart ailments. Scientific studies have supported tradition: the extract from combined parts of the tree can be used to treat chronic congestive heart failure, high blood pressure, and poor circulation. Just as the hawthorn has a dark side in mystical tradition, it also has its chemical complexities. Although its berries, or haws, are edible and make a great jelly, the seeds are poisonous: they contain cyanide bonded with sugar—amygdalin—which becomes hydrogen cyanide in the small intestine.

Cedar

The cedar tree was the inspiration for one of the oldest recorded works of world literature: the *Epic of Gilgamesh*, an ancient Mesopotamian poem that dates from the Third Dynasty of Ur, or about 2100 BCE. In it, Gilgamesh, king of the Sumerian city of Urek, journeys to the Cedar Forest to slay the ogre demi-god Humbaba. The cedar is also mentioned in Homer's *Iliad*, and it's said that the Apadana Palace of Persepolis (c.500 BCE) and the Temple of Solomon in Jerusalem (c.832 BCE) featured its wood. The cedar tree is considered sacred by many religions. The ancient Egyptian god Ra and the legendary Thunderbird revered by Native American Lakotas were said to live among cedars. The cedars of Lebanon, or cedars of God, have been an emblem of Lebanon since ancient times, when their timber was exploited by the Phoenicians, Assyrians, Babylonians, and Persians.

This spicy scented wood is also said to be the material from which the Ark of the Covenant was constructed, and perhaps even the cross upon which Jesus was crucified. The ancient Egyptians built ships with it, and in the nineteenth century, the Ottomans used it in railroad construction. Durable and rot-resistant, fragrant cedar is sought after today for musical instruments, ships, sacred and funerary religious objects, closets, hope chests, even longbows. One of the primary uses for cedar now is in the manufacturing of pencils. It is the ideal wood for this purpose because it doesn't warp, lose shape, or splinter when sharpened—plus it smells lovely. The eastern red cedar was used for making pencils from the mid-nineteenth century until about 1920. In the early twentieth century, American supplies of red cedar were so depleted that manufacturers even recycled cedar fences and barns to make pencils. They then made the switch to incense cedar, which is more plentiful and sustainable.

FROM OGRES AND PALACES TO NOTEBOOKS

Ancient yet constantly renewed, the cedar tree has many stories to tell. The next time you pick up a pencil, before you begin to write, pause for a moment and think about the cedar tree from which it came—scented like spice and sunlight, and revered since time immemorial.

There they stood, lofty arose the forest, and (astonished) they gazed at the height of the cedars and at the entrance of the cedar wood, where Humbaba was wont to walk with lofty steps. Ways were laid out and paths well kept. They saw the cedar hill, the dwelling of gods, the sanctuary of Ernini. In front of the hill (mountain) a cedar stood of great splendour, fine and good was its shade, filling with gladness [the heart].

From the ancient Mesopotamian poem *Epic of Gilgamesh,* translated by William Muss-Arnolt

Yew

The oldest existing manmade wooden object is believed to be a Paleolithic spear crafted from yew. Found in Clacton-on-Sea, England, by the archaeologist Samuel Hazzledine Warren in 1911, it is approximately 400,000 years old. This Clacton spear helps to put our associations with the yew tree into perspective. The Greeks and Romans used its wood for bows, as did archers in medieval England. It was a good choice because yew is a fine-grained, strong but flexible wood and is quite water-resistant.

Although known as the tree of life, the yew has long been linked to the sacred and to death. The Celts believed yew trees were gates to the other world. During the Middle Ages, yew trees became a popular choice for planting in holy places. In 1307, Edward I had them planted in churchyards to protect the church buildings from storms. Since that time, they have also been planted in cemeteries. The witches in Shakespeare's *Macbeth* added "gall of goat, and slips of yew" to their brew, which is logical because every part of this slow-growing tree, except for the bright red berry, or aril, that holds the seed, is poisonous. Yet the bark, which contains taxane, is used to make the cancer drug Taxol (paclitaxel), so

Of vast circumference and gloom profound,
This solitary Tree! A living thing
Produced too slowly ever to decay;
Of form and aspect too magnificent
To be destroyed.

From "Yew-Trees" by William Wordsworth
(1770–1850)

SEEING THE GOOD

Poisonous yet healing, ancient yet constantly renewed, the yew's wisdom is one of optimism. When everything seems impossible, remember that sometimes our best healing and understanding can come out of our darkest moments. In poison, there is medicine; in an ancient tree, there is growth.

perhaps "tree of life" isn't such a misnomer. Taxane is especially prevalent in yew trees found in the American Pacific Northwest.

There's another reason to associate the yew with hope for the future. The tree can live for thousands of years, and there are many famous examples still growing, such as the yews in Fortingall (Scotland) and Bermiego (Spain), as well as the remaining three of the "fraternal four of Borrowdale" in England, described by William Wordsworth as his poem continues:

Joined in one solemn and capacious grove;
Huge trunks! and each particular trunk a growth
Of intertwisted fibres serpentine
Up-coiling, and inveterately convolved…

Because of the layering process whereby yew branches touching the ground create new roots at the point of contact, and also the way in which the yew can renew itself from the outside inward—growing new outer layers as the inner layers of heartwood are rotting—it makes sense that this is also a tree associated with resurrection. According to Fred Hageneder in his book *The Spirit of Trees* (2005), "There is no biological reason for a yew tree to die—it can virtually live forever."

Rowan

Except, perhaps, for the mango, I don't think there's another tree that has quite as many names as the rowan, among them tree of bards, quickbeam, whitty pear, service tree, sorb apple, dogberry, and lady of the mountain. A relatively small tree—reaching up to forty feet high and twelve inches in diameter—it grows primarily in the mountains. It has also been called the wayfarer's tree or traveler's tree in the belief that it helped to prevent people from getting lost. Other names, such as witchwood, witchbeam, wikentree, witchen tree, and wicky, are nearly as myriad as the legends about how the rowan warded off witches and protected those people who trusted in it.

Rowan is one of the trees associated with the Celtic goddess and Christian Saint Brigid, the patron saint of the arts, scholars, poets, healers, and dairy workers, as well as weavers and spinners. That perhaps explains why in Scotland and Ireland spinning wheels were traditionally made of rowan wood.

According to British lore, the rowan offered protection from enchantment and witches, perhaps because it bears such a bright red fruit in the autumn. The color red has often been credited with such powers: in feng shui, it is used to repel negative energy, and in European cultures, red ribbon or coral is used to ward off the evil eye. The rowan's vibrant display of berries attracts birds, and may have inspired the red in many Scottish tartans. These berries, or pomes, end in a small five-pointed star that resembles a pentagram, a symbol long associated with protection from evil.

Making an amulet by tying two small twigs of rowan into the shape of a cross with red thread is an ancient tradition. These charms were hung on houses, barns, and even livestock to guard against evil. Brides sometimes sewed small amulets into their wedding dresses. With the crosses came a traditional saying: *Rowan tree and red thread make the witches tine [lose] their speed.*

A tree of wicken, as the rowan is called in the Lincolnshire fens, is marvellously effective against witches and all other ill things.

Mabel G. W. Peacock, folklorist (1856–1920)

Oak

Even the sound of the word "oak" evokes steadfastness and trust, perhaps of the self. A tree associated with that kind of endurance would seem to be a logical choice for a national tree, and the United States, Germany, Serbia, Cyprus, England, Estonia, France, Moldova, Romania, Jordan, Latvia, Lithuania, Poland, Wales, Galicia, and Bulgaria concur.

Myths and legends about the oak abound. It was considered sacred to the Greek god Zeus and to gods in ancient Middle Eastern, Slavic, Estonian, Norse, Celtic, Saxon, Greek, and Roman traditions. It's been associated with King Arthur and Robin Hood. In Welsh myths, the blossoms conjure magical realms. In many cultures, the oak tree is associated with heaven and hell, perhaps because of its roots, which are said to grow as deep as the tree is tall. The psychologist Carl Jung saw the oak tree as representative of a balanced self; the hidden roots as an apt metaphor for the unconscious. I wonder if the oak's lobed leaves that evoke the shape of the brain prompted that choice as well?

I was taken with the story of the Jackson Oak in Athens, Georgia, "The Tree that Owns Itself." A stone tablet near the oak bears a summary of a transaction initiated by Colonel William H. Jackson in the early nineteenth century:

For and in Consideration
Of the Great Love I Bear
This Tree and the Great Desire
I Have for its Protection
For All Time, I Convey Entire
Possession of Itself and
All Land Within Eight Feet
Of the Tree on All Sides

Jackson treasured his memories of playing under the tree as a child, and wanted to protect it and the land where it grew, so he deeded the tree to itself. It was uprooted in a windstorm in 1942, but a replacement, the "Son of the Tree that Owns Itself," was cultivated from a seedling from the original tree.

THE SELF AND SELFLESSNESS

The oak imparts wisdom about the self and selflessness. Take responsibility for our actions, own and know ourselves, and remember that even after we're gone, the acorns we planted will have grown into oaks.

He who plants an oak looks forward to future ages, and plants for posterity. Nothing can be less selfish than this. He cannot expect to sit in its shade nor enjoy its shelter; but he exults in the idea that the acorn which he has buried in the earth shall grow up into a loft pile, and shall keep on flourishing and increasing, benefiting mankind long after he shall have ceased to tread his paternal fields.

From *Bracebridge Hall* by Washington Irving, writer (1783–1859)

PART II

BRANCHES

Symbols, Myths, and Rituals

When I started posting photographs of the Red Hook Tree on Facebook, I was stunned at how many people responded—people I might have thought couldn't have cared less, or who had no connection with trees or even much of one with me. I think that is because just as almost every tree is sacred to someone, so every tree is a symbol of something. Trees in general represent strength, fecundity, and life, while many stand for something specific. But if you pay enough attention, all trees have meaning. For me, my maple has become a symbol of home and sanctuary, but especially connection. I look out of the window and I realize that almost all people have a tree or trees in their lives.

Dendrology is the study of trees. It's a compound word. The first part comes from the Greek and means "to be firm, solid, steadfast," and the second half, *ology*, indicates "the study of." Branches are usually the first thing we notice and what most people identify with when they think of trees. Yet, many trees (and their branches) represent the unseen: the mysteries of the acacia, the language of the beech, the lesson of the dogwood, and the timelessness of the poplar. Others are more like the apple, pear, and holly—familiar trees with perhaps surprisingly symbolic histories. The myths behind some trees make them truths for our lives: the alder for nurturing, the banyan for grounding, the fir for appreciating the present, and the sycamore for ensuring our own growth. Then there's the teak, and how the ritual of protecting it becomes a prayer of protection for the entire forest.

I read somewhere that there are over three *trillion* trees on Earth, which means about four hundred trees for each person. It's a never-ending pleasure to think of all the rituals—both large and small—that they inspire, the many things they represent, and the stories behind them.

The sacred tree, the sacred stone, are not adored as stone or tree; they are worshiped precisely because they are hierophanies, because they show something that is no longer stone or tree but the sacred…

Mircea Eliade, philosopher and historian (1907–1986)

Teak

Buddhist "forest" monks in Southeast Asia combine their ancient spiritual traditions with modern practicality by ordaining trees in much the same way as one might ordain a priest. Buddhists believe that we are all interrelated and interdependent—and that doesn't mean just people but all of creation, from animals to insects, oceans to forests. If we harm any of these beings, we harm ourselves.

The monks hold a ceremony and consecrate trees in areas threatened by logging, clear-cutting, and development by "dressing" the trees in sacred orange vestments that resemble the monks' own robes. They are hoping to prevent *Waldsterben*, a German word meaning "forest-death." After the ritual ends, the robes remain. Although this practice is rooted in an ancient belief in tree spirits, it sends a modern message about protecting our forests. It is a tactic to encourage loggers to pause before revving up their chainsaws. This is especially important when it comes to clear-cutting forests of valuable hardwoods, such as teak. It seems to work: environmentalists have seen this humble action have a significant impact.

Although there's always beauty in ritual, we can take a simpler and perhaps quieter approach as we choose a tree to ordain. Maybe it's a favorite place to sit in a park, a welcome landmark on the drive to work, or a promise of mangos every summer. All we need to do is deem that chosen tree sacred.

SAYING A PRAYER

Bring your own interpretation to the prayers that forest monks say for ordained trees. Vow to protect the trees of the forest and the city, the farm and the alley. Instead of cutting trees down, defend and protect them. Instead of ignoring them as mere scenery, truly see and appreciate them for the wisdom and healing they silently impart.

The Forest is a peculiar organism of unlimited kindness and benevolence, that makes no demands for its sustenance and extends generously the products of its activities; it affords protection to all beings, offering shade even to the axeman who destroys it.

Attributed to the Buddha on a sign in the New Forest National Park, Hampshire, England

Apple

I think that as we grow older we become more curious about what came before, and more concerned about what endures. Near my house is an apple tree that is about a century old. It's gnarled and half-dead, with large sections of peeling bark, but, stubbornly and miraculously, it still produces a healthy crop of apples, creating a fairytale woodland scene in the middle of an industrial block. Like the neighborhood, the block is being gentrified, and the lot where the apple tree grows is for sale. I suspect this will be the tree's last year.

From the Garden of Eden to Snow White, the apple has endured as a symbol of temptation. Even its Latin name, *Malus*, implies trouble, so perhaps there's a purpose to this tempting? As Thor Hanson wrote in *The Triumph of Seeds* (2015), "In nature, fleshy fruits of all kinds evolved for the sole purpose of tempting animals into dispersing the seeds of plants." I'm tempted to buy that lot—and if I had a limitless bank account, I would—and just let the tree be. I don't have that option, so instead my plan is to pick some of the fruit this fall, save the seeds, and see if I can continue the tree in another location—or two.

For many, such as the nineteenth-century American conservationist John Chapman, aka Johnny Appleseed, who traveled the Midwest planting apple tree nurseries, the apple is also a symbol of resurrection and rebirth. Ancient European cultures believed that the return of apple blossom symbolized the resurrection of nature. Demeter, the Greek goddess of the harvest and fertility, is also called "the apple bearer." According to folklore recounted by Sir James Frazer in *The Golden Bough* (1922), "Among the Kara-Kirghiz [Turkic peoples] barren women roll themselves on the ground under a solitary apple-tree, in order to obtain offspring."

The Lord is good to me,
And so I thank the Lord,
For giving me the
things I need,
The sun and the rain
and the apple seed.

Traditional North
American blessing

FROM A SEED TO A SYMBOL

Planting a tree can span the space between what came before and what will endure beyond. Try planting apple seeds, perhaps from a special tree or the remnants of a memorable lunch. First, germinate them on damp paper towels. Once they sprout, plant them in healthy soil where they can endure many generations of coming and going, building and abandonment. If you want your tree to produce apples, research how to graft a branch to the rootstock of another apple tree. Who knows what memory or what symbol your tree will create for someone else?

Beech

There's a reason we *leaf* through books. According to the Dictionary of Etymology, the Old English word *boc*, meaning "book," "writing," or any written document, shares its roots with the German *Buch*, with both words derived from "beech", as in the tree. This may be because early runes were inscribed on beech-wood tablets, or because people carved their wishes onto beech sticks or into the trees themselves—as young lovers used to do before people knew better. Some believe that the first books were made from thinly sliced panels of beech wood that were bound together.

There are many connections between beeches, all trees, writing, and language. The Latin word *codex* translates as "manuscript" but it originally meant "block of wood." The Latin for book, *liber*—the root of the word "library"—originally meant "tree bark," which was also used as an early writing material. Early texts such as the Pali Canon, the primary collection of Buddhist scriptures, were written on palm leaves. Native Americans, particularly the Ojibwa, wrote on birch-bark scrolls. The pages you are touching had their origins in a tree.

The word "paper" comes from the Latin *papyrus* and the Greek *papyros*—terms used for both the plant and the paper made from it that we generally associate with the ancient Egyptians. Nowadays, most paper is made from wood pulp, although to reduce waste and minimize deforestation, more recycled paper is being produced. Organizations such as the Book Industry Environmental Council (BIEC) are working to reduce the industry's environmental footprint. I, for one, hope they succeed, but I am still a big fan of books with pages to turn and mark, and between them press my favorite leaves from trees.

THE WRITER'S TREE

Trees as a vehicle for words have inspired writers since the beginning of written language. I like to think of the beech as the writer's tree. Take a little time to write with a pen or pencil on paper about a favorite tree that inspires you. Perhaps make a regular ritual of it for a few weeks. What do you see? How does the tree change over time? What can you learn from your words that are written on paper that came from a tree?

I frequently tramped eight or ten miles through the deepest snow to keep an appointment with a beech-tree, or a yellow birch, or an old acquaintance among the pines.

From *Walden* by Henry David Thoreau, American transcendentalist (1817–1862)

Poplar

In 1884, Richard Folkard wrote in *Plant Lore, Legends, and Lyrics* of the striking distinction between the opposing sides of the leaves of the white poplar, which are silver-white underneath and dark green on top. This difference in color caused the leaves to become a symbol of time, with the dark side representing night, and the light side day. Louise Cortambert, who wrote *The Language of Flowers* in 1834 under the name Charlotte de Latour, concurred, although her reasoning was a bit different. She wrote, "The ancients consecrated it to Time, because the leaves of this beautiful tree are in continual movement; and, brown on one side and white on the other, they indicate alternate day and night." In Greek and Roman mythology, poplar leaves symbolized death and life, or the underworld and the living world.

Time in tree terms is very different from human time. Trees have their own cycles and schedule. Poplars are considered one of the fastest-growing trees, adding five to eight feet to their height each year. Depending on the type and the environment, they can live from 100 to 450 years. Contrast that with cedars, which grow far more slowly—between one and two feet per year on average—and can live for two thousand years. Consider some of the oldest trees on our planet, such as redwoods that are more than three thousand years old, or bristlecone pines that have been on Earth for *five* thousand years!

Here is one of my favorites now before me, a fine yellow poplar, quite straight, perhaps 90 feet high, and four thick at the butt. How strong, vital, enduring! how dumbly eloquent! What suggestions of imperturbability and being, as against the human trait of mere seeming. Then the qualities, almost emotional, palpably artistic, heroic, of a tree; so innocent and harmless, yet so savage. It is, yet says nothing.

From "The Lesson of a Tree" in *Specimen Days* by Walt Whitman, American essayist and poet (1819–1892)

TREES AND TIME

Trees have a different chronology from humans and can teach us a lot about not squandering our lives. Simply look at a tree. It would be wonderful if it is a poplar, but any tree will do. Think about its history, its chronology, and compare it to yours. Try to remember a tree you've known all your life. Perhaps it was as tall as you were when you helped to plant it as a child, and now it towers over a house, a neighborhood. Imagine living your life at a tree's pace.

Alder

A symbiotic relationship exists between the alder tree and *Frankia alni*, a bacterium that resides in the tree's root nodules. The bacterium absorbs nitrogen from the air, releasing it into the tree, and the alder reciprocates by supplying the bacterium with sugars to sustain it. Most plants require nitrogen for growth, and the alder provides it for its neighbors, releasing it into the soil. For this reason, it is considered a pioneer species, and is often the first tree to grow in a damaged ecosystem, such as after clear-cutting or a fire. Alder is used for reforestation projects because it creates a fertile environment in which other trees can take root. It is one of the trees responsible for turning hundreds of acres of forest in Washington State green again after they were destroyed by the eruption of Mount St. Helen's in 1980.

Alders don't just feed the soil; they also provide sustenance for many creatures. Their catkins—the long clusters of tiny flowers that look a bit like caterpillars—are eaten by birds, rabbits, rodents, and numerous butterflies and moths. Some say alders are better at attracting butterflies and moths, including the spectacular mourning cloak butterfly and the luna moth, than the butterfly bush, or buddleia. About 140 varieties of insect are nourished by alder leaves. The tree also plays host to many species of moss, lichen, fungus, and bacterium beyond *Frankia alni*, and because alders grow in boggy ground, marshes, and near water, they provide shade by lakes and streams, and shelter for fish and other aquatic creatures.

The alder's typical proximity to water means that its wood is especially resistant to decay when wet. That's why it was used for the pilings for the Rialto Bridge in Venice and several of the city's medieval churches and cathedrals. A line written by the Roman poet Virgil (70–19 BCE)—"Then did the rivers feel the hollowed alders"—is often cited as evidence that the ancient boats, or at least canoes, were made from alder. The wood is now generally used to stabilize riverbanks, as the root system strengthens the shoreline, providing flood control and protecting the surrounding area.

NURTURING THE NURTURER

To honor all that the alder does for our ecosystem, do something for the alder. For me, the alder symbolizes nurturing, as it provides sustenance for so many species and shelter and security for even more. If you can find one, see if it needs *your* nurturing. Perhaps you could give it an offering of a good watering during a dry season, or explain to someone why it should be respected. Even if you can't find an alder, do something in your own way to nurture the natural world around you.

The alder, whose fat shadow nourisheth
Each plant set neere him long flourisheth.

From *Britannia's Pastorals* by William Browne (c.1590–c.1645)

Acacia

When he who was weary, plucked at a sprig of acacia, he had "evidence of things not seen."

From the November 1932 *Short Talk Bulletin,* Masonic Service Association of North America

While I can't pretend to know the secrets or complexities of freemasonry, that centuries-old fraternal order, self-described as a "beautiful system of morality, veiled in allegory and illustrated by symbols," I was drawn to the meaning that freemasons invest in the acacia. They lay it on the graves of their deceased members as an emblem of hope for the afterlife, choosing the acacia because its cut branches can sprout even when its roots are gone—a symbol of the immortal soul.

Much of the freemasons' connection to the tree comes from ancient texts. In Greek, *akakia* means "thorny Egyptian tree," and it is indeed native to Egypt. The sacred barge of Osiris, god of the afterlife, was built from acacia, as was the Ark of the Covenant. According to the Book of Exodus in the Bible, God appeared to Moses at the site of a burning bush, which biblical scholars believe was the acacia. Moses received instructions to lead the Israelites out of Egypt and into Canaan. Exodus goes on to tell how God instructed Moses to "make an ark" and "a table of acacia wood." This Ark of the Covenant, or chest, was believed to contain and conceal the tablets of the Ten Commandments, and perhaps other sacred objects as well.

Many varieties of acacia contain N,N-Dimethyltryptamine, or DMT. An hallucinogenic compound of the tryptamine family, DMT is used in shamanic rituals and is said to induce visions as well as near-death experiences. It is an ingredient in the psychoactive brew ayahuasca, or yagé, traditionally consumed by indigenous peoples of Amazonian Peru for divination and healing purposes. More recently, it has become a tool throughout the world for those seeking spiritual revelations.

The bullhorn acacia has another fascinating property. This tree, which is deficient in the unpleasant-tasting alkaloids that protect foliage from being eaten by insects and animals, lives in symbiosis with *Pseudomyrmex* ants. They inhabit the tree's hollowed thorns, remaining hidden until the tree is threatened. When it is, they release an alarm pheromone and emerge from the thorns to defend the tree. In return, the bullhorn acacia supplies the ants with protein-lipid nodules, called Beltian bodies, from its leaves, and with nectar from its leaf stalks. The sole purpose of these Beltian bodies is to nourish the ants.

Holly

The holly tree has long been a symbol of Christmas. Holly is used for decoration over the winter holidays because of its foliage, which remains dense even in cold weather, and its festive red berries (which are not actually berries, but drupes). Even before Christianity, holly wreaths were hung on doors and branches brought into homes to repel the evil eye and witches.

Some think the Holly King was an early precursor of Santa Claus. As a symbol of winter, he was said to rule over nature from the summer to the winter solstice. Then the Oak King defeated the Holly King to reign until the summer solstice returned.

There's another interesting link between oak and holly: oak draws lightning, while holly repels it. Many trees—the rowan, the hazel, and especially the holly—are traditionally described as "lightning trees". The ancient Roman historian Pliny the Elder wrote in his *Naturalis Historia* that holly around a house would protect it from lightning, and there are British legends to support this belief. Similarly, the French traditionally fastened holly branches against their walls as protection.

Studies by the Bartlett Tree Research Laboratories in Charlotte, North Carolina, seem to support this theory. They describe the susceptibility of the oak as "high" and of the holly as "low" for drawing lightning, explaining that some tree species are thought to be more receptive to it than others, although the reason for this is not known. It most likely has to do with tree height and the electrical conductivity of each species. There are many authors, from Victorian naturalists onward, who claim that the reason holly can repel lightning is because of the thorns on its spiky leaves, which dissipate electrical charges. But, search as I might, I couldn't find vetted research to support this.

POWER AND BEAUTY

I think there's poetry to a tree that we can bring into our homes to provide green in gray winters, and which can offer protection from elements beyond our control. Take a moment to consider not just the beauty of the holly tree but also how science and legend can connect— those places where symbols of the mystical and objective research overlap.

The holly and the ivy,
When they are both full grown,
Of all the trees that are in the wood,
The holly bears the crown.

From the traditional Christmas carol published in *English Folk-Carols*, collected by Cecil B. Sharp (1911)

Banyan

In Sanskrit, the banyan is called the "tree of many feet" because of the way its many roots spread. There are several famous banyan trees, especially in India. One in particular, on a bank of India's Nerbudda River and reputedly planted by the fifteenth-century poet and saint Kabir, was long believed to be the oldest in the country, until it was destroyed by flood. Another spectacular example is Thimmamma Marrimanu (*marri* means "banyan," and *manu* "tree" in Telugu) in the Indian state of Andhra Pradesh. According to Guinness World Records, it is the world's biggest banyan, with branches spreading over five acres, and a canopy of almost 23,000 square yards. It's so vast that a small Hindu temple has been built within its massive trunk. The banyan, which is sacred in Hinduism, is often depicted with the god Shiva sitting under its canopy, and saints gathered at his feet.

Mentioned in books by many nineteenth-century naturalists, the banyan has continued to inspire in recent times. Mahatma Gandhi created the term Satyagraha, loosely translated as "polite insistence on the truth." He wrote in 1919: "Satyagraha is like a banyan tree… *Satya* (truth) and *ahimsa* (non-violence) together make the present trunk from which innumerable branches shoot out… We must fearlessly spread the doctrine of *satya*

and *ahimsa*, and then, and not till then, shall we be able to undertake mass *satyagraha*." This form of non-violent resistance influenced many, including Martin Luther King, Jr., during the American Civil Rights Movement, and Nelson Mandela in his struggle against apartheid in South Africa.

GROUND YOURSELF

Like the non-violent protester, the banyan will not be moved. It is grounded and fixed to the earth by a multitude of connections. Be like the banyan by trying the tree pose from yoga. Standing, concentrating on feeling grounded and your gaze fixed forward, lift a foot and place it on the opposite thigh. Bring your hands together on your chest as if in prayer and consider the banyan tree soaring upward yet always rooted.

In the forest of India is found a tree of the fig tribe called the Banyan. All the branches of this tree naturally bend to the earth, and push their way downward. When they are long enough to reach the ground they take root, and soon grow into strong trunks, until in the process of time the aged banyan becomes chained to the earth by ten hundred ties.

From *Rays from the Realms of Nature* by Reverend James Neil,
19th-century British author and explorer

Fir

Although the maple is the heart of this book, for me the fir is very much a "Be More Tree" tree, a mindfulness tree. There's a lot to love about the fir. Its balsam fragrance evokes Christmas morning and hiking in the mountains after rainfall. Its lively cones close up in rain and open in sunny weather. For me, the fir also evokes a story I heard as a child and have never quite forgotten.

Hans Christian Andersen's fairy tale *The Fir Tree* is the heartbreaking account of a young fir growing in the woods. Its world was lovely but the sunlight and the birds—the present moment—weren't enough for it. It wanted to grow taller and become older, certain that would be the "most delightful thing in the world!" The fir tree did grow, but then it wanted to fly like the swallows, or have adventures like the other trees in the woods—the ones the woodcutters felled and took away. What became of them?

After several years, the tree found out: it was cut down, covered with tinsel, tapers, and treats, and made into a family's Christmas tree. The fir was delighted by the celebration, stories, and splendor until the day after Christmas, when it was relegated to a dark corner of the attic with only mice and rats for company. Hope was renewed in the spring when one morning the tree was brought outside, back into the sunlight, but its joy didn't last. Merry children removed the last bits of tinsel and a gardener chopped the tree into firewood. If only the fir had been more tree…

BEING IN THE MOMENT

Hans Christian Andersen's story teaches us to appreciate the present moment, just as it is. It's not that difficult to find a fir tree—they grow throughout much of North and Central America, Europe, Asia, and North Africa—so do your best. Now, be more tree! Sit with it. Truly look at it. Inhale its aroma. Experience its textures, its shade, and its presence. Try to shut out everything but the fir and be with it, just as it is and just as you are.

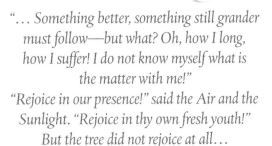

"… Something better, something still grander must follow—but what? Oh, how I long, how I suffer! I do not know myself what is the matter with me!"
"Rejoice in our presence!" said the Air and the Sunlight. "Rejoice in thy own fresh youth!" But the tree did not rejoice at all…

From *The Fir Tree* by Hans Christian Andersen, author (1805–1875), translated by Charles Boner

Sycamore

It is said that Thoth, the ancient Egyptian god of writing, wrote the names of pharaohs on sycamore trees—more specifically, *Ficus sycomorus*, also called Pharaoh's fig— and that this action guaranteed the rulers' immortality. The Egyptian Book of the Dead mentions the tree: "I embraced the sycamore and the sycamore protected me…," and, accordingly, it was planted near tombs to protect the deceased. Legend has it, in ancient Rome, Cicero and his cohorts were so taken with a sycamore that they poured wine instead of water onto its roots.

Herodotus, a Greek historian from the fifth century BCE, wrote that the Persian king Xerxes, while marching his thousands of troops from Phrygia to Sardis, came upon a sycamore so beautiful that he fell a little in love with it. He stopped his campaign for three days, luxuriated in its shade, and decorated it with precious ornaments. When he continued, he left a guard behind to protect the tree, and had its image wrought upon a golden medallion that he would wear for the rest of his life.

The sycamore's power to transform is also mentioned in the Bible. The Gospel according to Luke relates how the tax collector Zacchaeus climbed a sycamore so that he could see Jesus as he passed by. After Jesus announced that he would be visiting Zacchaeus's house, he let Jesus's teachings into his heart and came down from the tree an honest man.

This sycamore of ancient texts—*Ficus sycomorus*—is a distant relative of the tree of which American authors wrote, such as John Steinbeck in *Of Mice and Men* and Kate Chopin in *The Awakening*, and is not the one of Native American lore—that's *Platanus occidentalis*, the buttonwood. *Ficus sycomorus* is a little more closely related to the London plane tree (*Platanus × acerifolia*, syn. *Platanus × hispanica*), a hybrid that was planted throughout London during the Industrial Revolution because of its resistance to pollution. It is believed that the tree's rapidly flaking bark helps it to slough off pollutants.

The sycamore changed the warrior king Xerxes into a tree-hugging naturalist, Zacchaeus into an honest man, the pharaohs of Egypt into cohorts of the gods, and the air of London into something breathable. Whether a *Ficus* or a *Platanus*, the sycamore is a symbol of transformation.

HONORING TRANSFORMATION

Celebrate a tree and how it can change you. How were you different before that tree came into your life? Is there a tree you like to spend time with as you meditate, think, or seek change?

The branches of the great sycamore tree wove themselves into the stitch of the sky like crooked threads.

From *The Way* (2012) by Kristen Wolf, author

Dogwood

According to a number of legends, Jesus's cross was made of dogwood, chosen because the timber is very dense and sturdy. Some also say that the tree from which the wood was harvested was once the largest in Jerusalem, but that after his crucifixion, Jesus shrunk it and twisted its branches so that it could never again be used for making crosses. Even though the dogwood probably didn't grow in biblical lands at the time, this makes for a poignant story.

What we call the dogwood flower is actually the bract: the "leaves" that contain and protect the tiny flowers within. Poinsettia plants have a similar construction. Dogwood bracts are cross-shaped, or cruciform, and each has a stain of red, which is said to represent a rusty bloodstain from a crucifixion nail. The flower stamens in the very center of each bract represent a tiny crown of thorns—another reminder of how Jesus suffered.

Dogwoods develop different growth patterns depending on where they are. Woodland dogwoods are mono-layered, their branches arranged in alternating layers so that none ever shades the branch growing below it. In this way, each flower is exposed equally to sunlight. In contrast, dogwoods that grow in sunnier locations, where competition for sunlight is not a problem, tend to be multilayered, their branches overlapping so that those beneath are protected from too much exposure. To me, this is empathy, as if the branches tended to one another.

GOING BEYOND OURSELVES

The dogwood teaches us about having concern for the suffering of others. Pause to think about what kind of impact our actions have on others. How can we learn from the dogwood?

...But high o'er all the early floral train,
Where softness all the arching sky resumes,
The dogwood dancing to the winds' refrain,
In stainless glory spreads its snowy blooms.

From "Dogwood Blossoms" by George Marion McClellan, poet (1860–1934)

Pear

According to *The Language of Flowers* (1834), written by Louise Cortambert under the name Charlotte de Latour, pear blossoms symbolize comfort. To that I would add survival. In his documentary film *The Trees*, Scott Elliott chronicles the progress of the trees planted at the National September 11 Memorial Plaza at Ground Zero in New York, and the lives of the people who tend to them. Among all those trees and their remarkable stories, there is a Callery pear that is especially remarkable.

Callery pears are good city street trees because they grow straight up and don't require much care. One such tree was very close to the World Trade Center when the towers fell on September 11, 2001. The 9/11 Survivor Tree, or the "Tree that Would Not Be Broken," is a thirty-year-old Callery pear. When the New York City Parks Department rescued it from the debris ten months after the planes hit, it was damaged, seemingly mortally wounded. Still, it was brought to Van Cortlandt Park in the Bronx, where Richie Cabo, a horticulturist with the Parks Department, tended to it. Ron Vega, the director of design and construction at the memorial, heard about the pear tree and tracked it down—he believed it was an important symbol of survival.

In 2010, Cabo and Vega returned the tree to Lower Manhattan and the site of New York's newly built National September 11 Memorial Plaza, where it's currently thriving. There's no plaque or mention of the Survivor Tree in guidebooks, but people seem drawn to it. With its new leaves, blossoms, and fruits, it represents regrowth and survival for New Yorkers and for everyone else who encounters it.

It took a long time for this tree to recover, just like Ground Zero. I had to fight back tears as I saw it come back home.

Ruth Mullen, author and editor (1953–)

A SYMBOL OF HOPE

If you look at photographs of the 9/11 Survivor Tree, you can see divisions in the bark—the lines between where it encountered death and where it began to grow again. Take inspiration from the pear, or from any tree. Even at the darkest moments of our lives, there is a seed, a blossom, new growth, and a hope for survival.

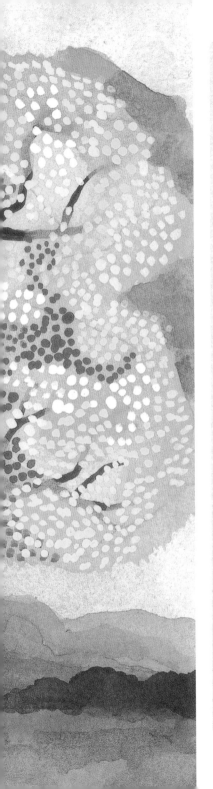

PART III
LEAVES

Healing, Science, and Practical Applications 72

Healing, Science, and Practical Applications

When I was eleven or twelve years old, I had a summer camp counselor who took us out into the woods and showed us things: how wintergreen picked along a path tasted better than chewing gum, how the roots of Queen Anne's lace could be eaten like carrots, the delicacy of fern fiddleheads. Mostly city children, we were amazed. The things that grew all around us had uses, purposes beyond ornament. They could feed us, heal us. Clearly, I never forgot the experience, and there was more to it. As we were chewing leaves and spitting grit from roots, the counselor hushed us and told us to look up to pay attention to how the wind swayed the tall Michigan pines, to watch the way aspens flipped their leaves to meet the rain and sun, and to think about the creatures that lived without human intervention or even notice in the forest canopy.

Leaves distinguish trees—each silhouette is distinctive of the species and is the best way to identify it. The science of trees spans medicine to ecology, and beyond. Just as every tree has a specific leaf identity, many trees heal in a specific way. We can bathe in birch essence or frankincense like royalty; be nourished by dates, ginkgo nuts, or linden flower honey; inhale eucalyptus steam and sip willow tea.

There is also healing that can't be seen, such as the memories evoked by the comforting scent of camphor; the incense of hickory; the energy, or *qi*, of the larch; the power of forest bathing among sugi trees; and the inspiration of ash and yucca to heal our planet and, ultimately, ourselves.

I've forgotten that camp counselor's name, but I'll never forget that day in the woods. Sometimes, when I'm troubled, I go outside and just look up at my maple tree. Sitting with it, inhaling the subtle fragrance of its greening in the spring or the headier scent of its decaying leaves in autumn, make me better. Sometimes tending to it heals me as well— it gets me outdoors to sweep up its seedpods and, especially, to rake its leaves in the autumn, perhaps my favorite contemplative practice. In his essay "Listening to Natural Law," Chief Oren Lyons of the Onondaga Nation wrote: "In the spring when the sap runs through the trees, we have ceremonies, thanksgiving. For the maple, chief of the trees, leader of all the trees, thanksgiving. Thanksgiving for all the trees." For me, the raking and the sweeping are a kind of thanksgiving.

I go to Nature to be soothed and healed, and to have my senses put in tune once more.

From *The Gospel of Nature* by John Burroughs, American naturalist (1837–1921)

Leaves • 73

Ash

Yggdrasil was the world tree in Scandinavian myths. An enormous ash, its roots reached the lairs of the gods, and its branches spread to the edges of the universe as it protected the Earth. Such powerful imagery, such a noble tree, but now the ash needs *our* protection.

According to Helen Macdonald in *The New York Times* in 2015, "ash dieback disease, a new and virulent fungal infection that has spread westward across Europe… will likely kill nearly all the ashes in Britain. In America, the effects of the invasive emerald ash borer beetle have been just as devastating. Globalization is the culprit… The accelerating scale and speed of international trade has brought numerous pathogens and pests to species with no natural resistance."

Why does this matter? What's one less tree? The point is that the environment is undergoing radical change. Think about the loss of over *one hundred million* ash trees in the United States in merely four years—that's the impact the ash borer beetle had. Then multiply it by all the trees on the planet and the many threats they face; this is as vast as the reach of Yggdrasil's limbs and roots.

A study published in the *American Journal of Preventive Medicine* in 2013 stated: "There was an increase in mortality related to cardiovascular and lower-respiratory-tract illness in counties infested with the emerald ash borer. The magnitude of this effect was greater as infestation progressed and in counties with above-average median household income. Across the 15 states in the study area, the borer was associated with an additional 6,113 deaths related to illness of the lower respiratory system, and 15,080 cardiovascular-related deaths." In conclusion, the health of these trees is directly related to the health of the people who share their environment.

In the wetlands along the St. Lawrence River in northern New York and Quebec, the Mohawk people of Akwesasne have made it their mission to protect the black ash from the emerald ash borer, overharvesting, and pollution. They collect, store, and plant seeds and educate people about the threats to the tree. One easy but

important lesson they teach is not to move firewood and inadvertently spread beetles and other non-indigenous pests. The black ash is integral to Mohawk heritage. The people have traditionally woven baskets from the wood, in a craft passed down through generations. By protecting the ash, they're protecting not only their culture and the wildlife that thrives in an ash forest, but our planet too.

The ash Yggdrasil suffers anguish,
More than men can know;
The stag bites above; on the side it rots;
And the dragon gnaws from beneath.

From *The Prose Edda* by Snorri Sturluson, Icelandic scholar (1179–1241), translated by Henry Adams Bellows

Willow

Since ancient times, willow bark has been used as a remedy for fevers and chills. Hippocrates prescribed it in 400 BCE, and the ancient Sumerians and Egyptians and the Native Americans chewed it for its curative properties. It worked because willow contains a chemical called salicin, an anti-inflammatory. As with any medication, however, there can be too much of a good thing; salicin is said to have contributed to the death of Beethoven, who ingested such large amounts that he damaged his kidneys.

In 1838, the Italian chemist Raffaele Piria derived a more potent form of willow extract, which he called salicylic acid. Felix Hoffmann and other chemists at the pharmaceutical company Bayer then synthesized acetylsalicylic acid in 1853, later dubbed "aspirin" by the company, creating the precursors to the white tablets we buy at the pharmacy today for aches and pains.

As this tree delights in a moist or wet soil, where agues chiefly abound, the general maxim, that many natural maladies carry their cures along with them, or that their remedies lie not far from their causes, was so very apposite to this particular case, that I could not help applying it…

From a letter to the Royal Society in 1763 written by Edmund Stone, vicar (1702–68)

MAKING WILLOW TEA

Many people find that willow tea is gentler on the stomach than commercial medication and has a longer-lasting effect. Either buy willow bark from an herbalist or a health food store, or try wildcrafting. In spring or early summer, carefully trim some young willow branches less than three inches in diameter from the tree. With a peeling knife, strip the bark from the pulp. Don't strip the bark directly from the tree, as this will harm it! Cut the bark into two-inch squares and dry at about 65°F (18°C) on a drying rack or in an oven. Crumble the bark, then simmer one to two teaspoons of it in one cup of water for fifteen minutes, and let steep for thirty minutes before drinking. Fresh ginger is believed to enhance the potency, and you'll probably want to add a sweetener such as honey because, although the effects are worthwhile, tea from willow bark tastes like…well, tree bark!

Sugi

The sugi tree (*Cryptomeria japonica*) is also known as the Japanese cedar, even though it is not a true cedar. Honored and considered sacred, it is the national tree of Japan, where it is protected if it is growing in or near a Buddhist temple or Shinto shrine. Some sugis are ancient, such as the Houkisugi at Nakagawa, said to be over two thousand years old, or Jōmon Sugi on the island of Yakushima, which is about five thousand years old. The sugi is a familiar image in Japanese decorative arts and woodblock prints, including the creations by the twentieth-century master of the craft Yoshida Hiroshi. It is also a favorite tree for bonsai—the art of replicating nature's beauty by growing and tending miniature trees.

In short, sugi trees are distinctly Japanese, and so is *Shinrin-Yoku*, which translates as "forest bathing." The name was coined by the Japanese government in the early 1980s, but *Shinrin-Yoku* is based on ancient meditation practices akin to mindfulness. According to an article published in 2009 by the immunologist Dr. Qing Li in *Environmental Health and Preventive Medicine*, "a forest bathing trip… is a short, leisurely visit to a forest and is regarded as being similar to natural aromatherapy. A forest bathing trip involves visiting a forest for relaxation and recreation while breathing in volatile substances, called phytoncides (wood essential oils), which are antimicrobial volatile organic compounds derived from trees, such as α-pinene [alpha-pinene] and limonene." The sugi is a prime source of these phytoncides, which have been proven to reduce blood pressure, heart rate, and the production of stress hormones. Phytoncides may even prevent certain cancers. Japan's forestry agency takes this research seriously: it has created over forty-eight official Forest Therapy trails.

How time-worn all
has grown, unnoticed!
On the hill of Kagu the
moss lies green
At the ancient roots
Of the speary cryptomerias.

From "Envoys" by Kamo Taruhito, eighth-century Japanese poet, translated by Nippon Gakujutsu Shinkōkai

PRACTICING FOREST BATHING

Try it yourself! As M. Amos Clifford writes in *A Little Handbook of Shinrin-Yoku* (2013), "It's not just about taking walks in the forest." Forest bathing means devoting yourself to being present in the forest and with trees—from sprout to decaying stump. Clear your mind. Relax your gaze and appreciate the play of the branch-filtered light. Feel the wind through the leaves. Listen to the sounds—not just the rustle and creak, but the quietude. Inhale the fragrance of the forest; exhale the serenity. Be still and be more tree.

Hickory

The word "hickory" is derived from *pawcohicora*, the Algonquin (or perhaps Powhatan) name for the oil derived from hickory nuts, which was mixed with bear grease and used as a salve. A member of the walnut family, the hickory comes in many nut-bearing varieties. When we in North America think of hickory, it is most often the shagbark hickory that comes to mind. The name is logical: the bark appears shaggy, tattered, and scruffy, as if it is about to fall from the tree in vertical strips. Native Americans gathered this bark, which the tree shed naturally, toasted it, and brewed a tea rich in magnesium and said to be good for arthritis.

With the current renewed interest in local and sustainable foods, hickory syrup—which can be produced from hickory sap without damaging the tree—is growing in popularity and is increasingly available at farmers' markets. This sweet syrup, which is similar to, but lighter than, maple syrup, is also believed to have healing and soothing properties.

However, not everything about the hickory is healing and nurturing. Hickories and other members of the walnut family secrete juglone, which is poisonous to other trees such as apple and birch, and even to other hickories. The chemical is released through the roots, the leaves that fall to the ground, through the shells of the nuts, and even from raindrops that have lingered in the trees' canopy. Its purpose is to weed out the competition for light and nourishment.

Hickory nuts are edible and similar to pecans, providing sustenance for humans and livestock alike. They're tasty when toasted or can be baked into bread. It often takes three or four decades for the trees to produce nuts—they need a very long taproot before they can bear them—but, fortunately, hickory trees can live for centuries.

Just as the hickory is a slow-growing tree, it is also a slow-burning tree. One of the most desirable firewoods, it burns a very hot 18.6 BTUs per cord (a unit of volume, equal to about 128 cubic feet), which is higher than most other woods. There is minimal smoke, but that which is produced has a most wonderful fragrance.

By beautiful I mean something allowed to become fully realized—a hickory leaf, for example, emerging after an uninterrupted process.

From *Slowspoke: A Unicyclist's Guide to America* (2013) by Mark Schimmoeller, author

HICKORY TIME

The hickory tree has much to teach us about perseverance, patience, and the healing power of taking our time. Find some dry hickory in the woods or buy some hickory chips. Take your time building a small fire, in a fireplace, brazier, or a safe spot outdoors. As you breathe in the sweet, spicy scent and observe the beauty of the burning wood, consider the long path it has taken to becoming charcoal, from pollen, seeds, sprouts, and seedlings to the seasons and years of growth. Then apply that sense of time, of patience, to your life. Recognize that healing—whether physical, emotional, or spiritual—like the growth of a hickory tree, can't all happen at once.

Date Palm

In medieval Europe, it was believed that drinking date palm wine from a unicorn's horn would cure illness and act as an antidote to poison. Perhaps, if we had access to a unicorn's horn, we could find out if that were true. What is far more certain is that the date palm is one of the oldest cultivated trees, growing throughout the Middle East and the Indus Valley, and it is mentioned more than fifty times in the Bible and twenty times in the Qur'an.

Dates have been a staple food for millennia. They were believed to cure a variety of ailments, and current research supports these ancient teachings. Highly nutritious, they are not only a good source of energy, but also contain the trace elements selenium, copper, potassium, and magnesium, C and B vitamins, fiber, antioxidants, carotenoids, and phenolics. The seeds contain protein and other nutrients.

If that weren't enough to award dates with the label of "superfood," the *Journal of Obstetrics and Gynaecology* recently published a study titled "The Effect of Late Pregnancy Consumption of Date Fruit on Labour and Delivery." Centuries after the story of the virgin birth, the authors concluded that "the consumption of date fruit in the last 4 weeks before labour significantly reduced the need for induction and augmentation of labour, and produced a more favourable, but non-significant, delivery outcome." The most gratifying part of the study was that the researchers observed that the latent phase of the early stage of labor was shorter for the date-eating mothers compared with the non-date-eaters by as much as six hours.

Possibly one of the longest gestation periods in the history of time was that of the Methuselah date palm in Ketura, Israel. In 2005, a young plant was coaxed out of a seed that had been recovered in 1963 from Masada, a fortress in present-day Israel, where in 70 CE Jewish zealots killed themselves to avoid capture by the Romans. It is incredible that a viable plant grew from a seed that was more than two thousand years old. At the time of writing, the tree stands more than ten feet tall and has produced pollen, which will fertilize more date palms when caught on the breeze.

DINING ON DATES

Dates are clearly a powerful fruit, so eat some! They are wonderful by themselves, chopped into a salad, or used in place of jam in a peanut butter sandwich. Date sugar is also an excellent substitute for refined white sugar. Consider how the depth of the flavor and the texture of the pith connect us to date-eaters throughout millennia.

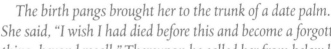

The birth pangs brought her to the trunk of a date palm. She said, "I wish I had died before this and become a forgotten thing, beyond recall." Thereupon he called her from below her [saying,] "Do not grieve! Your Lord has made a spring to flow at your feet. Shake the trunk of the palm tree, freshly picked dates will drop upon you. Eat, drink, and be comforted."

The Qur'an, Maryam 19:22–26

Birch

Celebrated in the poetry and prose of many great Russian writers, including Alexey and Leo Tolstoy, the birch is generally considered to be the national tree of Russia. It has also long been associated with Russian folk medicine.

The sweet, clear, watery sap, which is collected as winter wanes, before the tree goes to leaf, is a tonic that is good for the skin and hair. It is also thought to improve arthritis and joint pain. The bark and sap contain betulin, which has been shown to slow the growth of tumors and boost the immune system. And then, of course, there is the Russian steam bath: the *banya*.

The Russian and Eastern European equivalent of the Turkish *hamam*, Japanese *sentō*, Scandinavian sauna, and Native American sweat lodge, the *banya* is a ritual for community, health, and relaxation. Birch is an essential element of these steam baths. The firewood used to heat the cauldrons of bathwater is generally birch, and fresh birch leaves are placed over hot rocks to infuse the steam. Perspiring in the birch essence helps bathers to detoxify,

relieves aches, reduces stress, and, it is said, improves the immune system. After soaking in the steam and raising their body temperature, bathers strike themselves with *venik*, bundles of fresh birch or dried birch twigs moistened with hot water, which is believed to improve circulation.

Banya is also credited with widening the bronchial tubes, removing phlegm, and ventilating the lungs, which explains why it is easier to breathe afterward. Birch leaves apparently release phytocides, which kill or slow down the growth and development of pathogens, as well as essential oils, which improve the metabolism and stop the premature aging of the skin.

White gleamed the silver birches—
It was the morning of our life!
O happiness! O tears!
O life! O woods! O sunshine clear!
Fresh breath of silver birches.

From "It Was in the Early-Early Spring" by Alexey Tolstoy (1883–1945), translated by Nadine Jarintzov

SOAKING IN THE BIRCH

Not everyone has access to a Russian *banya*, but most people have access to birch trees. They flourish throughout the Northern Hemisphere and Asia, so it is possible to benefit from their healing properties. In the early summer, gather a shopping bag or so of fresh birch leaves. Rinse them well, then boil them for about two hours in a large pot with enough water to cover them. Simmering will release the essential oils. Strain the liquid, add it to a tub full of hot water, climb in, and soak. Perhaps you'll read the works of the great Russian poets as you luxuriate in your birch bath.

Frankincense

Native to the Arabian Peninsula and northeast Africa, the frankincense (*Boswellia*) tree is perhaps most familiar to Western readers from the New Testament, in which the resin from the frankincense tree was one of the treasures, along with gold and myrrh, offered to the infant Jesus by the three Magi. There's a long history to prizing gold, myrrh, and frankincense. The ancient Egyptian queen Hatshepsut, who reigned in the fifteenth century BCE, organized a famous expedition to the Land of Punt—believed to be in the area of what is now Somalia. According to archaeologists Edouard Naville and Howard Carter in *The Tomb of Hâtshopsîtû* (1906), the queen's men returned to Egypt with tribute including "gold in rings, a heap of boomerangs…and a big heap of frankincense" all depicted on the walls of her temple at Deir el Bahari. It has been said that she planted frankincense trees in the courtyards of the temple, and this seems to be true: Naville excavated intact frankincense roots, remnants of which can still be seen there today.

The resin of the frankincense tree is harvested by cutting shallow incisions in the bark and allowing the oily gum to seep out; it then turns into hard nodules, called tears. These are used for a variety of purposes. In Somalia, where most frankincense comes from, the resin is believed to bring good health, and it is burned in the home, producing a woody, fruity smell. It is also burned at Roman Catholic masses and Arab weddings.

Certain grades of frankincense resin and oil are edible and feature in traditional African and Asian medicines to aid digestion and promote healthy skin. In Indian Ayurvedic medicine, it is used to treat arthritis and hormonal problems. It is even said that the oil can heal scorpion stings. Frankincense is currently the subject of numerous scientific studies and trials for the treatment of everything from ulcerative to ovarian cancer, and osteoarthritis to depression.

Unfortunately, the frankincense tree is in danger, and it has been estimated that the number of trees could decline by 90 percent in the next fifty years. This is, in part, as a result of the trees being over-tapped to meet increased demand for the resin, but drought brought on by climate change has also had an impact and diminished their population. It is hoped that recent studies into the tree's sap-secreting system will help to reverse this trend.

HEALING GIFTS

Frankincense has been treasured by ancient queens and warriors, doctors and poets. Its oil is used by aromatherapists and sold by herbalists and in health food stores. Although the prices vary wildly, it is worth doing a little research and procuring a bottle. Put a few drops in a bathtub and soak in its ancient healing properties.

Hint of suppressed halo,
Rustle of hidden wings,
Wafture of heavenly frankincense,—

From "Angels" by Gertrude Hall (1863–1961)

Ginkgo

After maple and oak leaves, it was the ginkgo's fan-shaped leaves that I next learned to identify as a child. In the autumn, there's a distinctive scent in my neighborhood in Brooklyn, and in parks all over the planet, when the ginkgo trees drop their fruit.

The ginkgo is often described as a living fossil because its lineage dates back 270 million years to the Permian Era. Native to China, it is widely cultivated and has long been important in human history. It has various uses in traditional medicine and is a source of food. According to traditional Chinese medicine and *The Great Herbal* (1578) by Li Shih-chen, the fruit can be used to treat asthma, coughs, and bladder problems. The seeds, meanwhile, are prescribed for cancer and to help digestion.

Western sources concur that the ginkgo is a source of tremendous healing. It improves circulation and oxygenates the brain. According to Helen Farmer-Knowles in *The Healing Plants Bible* (2010), the leaves, fruit, and cooked seed can be used to treat allergies, asthma, vertigo, circulation and digestion problems, coughs, insomnia, fungus, pulmonary tuberculosis, and bronchitis. The Mayo Clinic in Minnesota agrees, and adds dementia, anxiety, schizophrenia, and altitude sickness to this impressive list.

*This tree, entrusted by the East
Unto my garden-ground, doth show
A leaf whose hidden sense can feast
Their hearts who are skilled to know.*

From "Gingo Biloba" [sic] by Johann Wolfgang von Goethe, poet and mystic (1749–1832), translated by Edward Dowden

GATHERING GINKGO

The ginkgo nut is a favorite of urban foragers. Harvest your own fruit in the autumn—you'll know it's ripe if it smells a bit like vomit—but wear rubber gloves in case you have a mild allergic reaction to them. Soak the fruits overnight until you can separate out the nuts inside. After rinsing the nuts, spread them on a cookie sheet and bake at 180°F (80°C) for about 45 minutes—they're ready when the shells are dry. Store them in an airtight container for weeks or toast them right away in a cast-iron skillet with a little oil and salt. Crack the shells and eat the nuts inside, which taste a bit like chestnuts. Don't eat more than six or seven per day—too many can be toxic—and never give them to small children.

Eucalyptus

When we think of eucalyptus, or gum, trees, we think of Australia, and koalas, possums, and other marsupial herbivores noshing on the leaves. We think of the spicy menthol fragrance of the leaves, which, when distilled to oil, can be used to create inhalants for lung or sinus congestion, incorporated into balms for muscle aches and arthritis, or used as an antibacterial cleanser.

The eucalyptus has another healing property that is also distinctively Australian: didgeridoo music. Didgeridoos—the wind instruments used for playing traditional Australian Aboriginal music—are made from eucalyptus wood. Whenever possible, they are carved to the appropriate size and shape from live wood, branches, or stems that have been hollowed out by termites. I love the fact that many contemporary didgeridoo craftspeople cut the eucalyptus trees in such a way that they'll resprout and grow again. Truly, no trees need be felled to make a didgeridoo! The sound the didgeridoo makes is haunting, somewhere between a human voice and a musical instrument. The Australian Aborigines believe the world was sung into being and that the music of the didgeridoo fosters spiritual healing because it intersects with the Dreaming, or *Jukurrpa*. Jeannie Herbert Nungarrayi (1953–2014), a lifelong teacher and champion of Warlpiri culture,

described it like this: "The *Jukurrpa* is an all-embracing concept that provides rules for living, a moral code, as well as rules for interacting with the natural environment. The philosophy behind it is holistic—the *Jukurrpa* provides for a total, integrated way of life."

It is not just the people of Australia, or shamans, or proponents of New Age practices who recognize the power of music. Neuroscientists such as Oliver Sacks concurred, as do traditional medical practitioners. This is exemplified by numerous articles and studies, including this excerpt from an article by J. M. White from 2001 in the journal *Nursing Clinics of North America*: "Music interventions have been used in medicine and nursing throughout history. Music therapy is an easy-to-administer, relatively inexpensive, noninvasive intervention that has been used to reduce heart rate, blood pressure, myocardial oxygen consumption, gastrointestinal function, anxiety, and pain." Remember that breathing itself is linked to healing, and playing the didgeridoo requires the technique of circular breathing. The healing power of music is universal. It is not just the didgeridoo that's meditative—so is the Indian sitar, the Japanese shakuhachi flute, the Persian santur, the Tibetan singing bowl, or any instrument played with contemplative intent.

The inexpressible depth of music, so easy to understand and yet so inexplicable, is due to the fact that it reproduces all the emotions of our innermost being, but entirely without reality and remote from its pain… Music expresses only the quintessence of life and of its events, never these themselves.

From *The World as Will and Representation* by Arthur Schopenhauer, philosopher (1788–1860), translated by E. F. J. Payne

Larch

Larches are spectacular trees with feathery foliage that turns a brilliant gold in the autumn. Although conifers, they are unusual in being deciduous: they drop their leaves before winter and grow fresh green shoots in the spring. Larch trees are found all over the planet, from the Rocky Mountains in America to the hills of Scotland, the Alps to the Urals, the Himalayas to the Taihang Mountains of China.

Larch is one of the fifty fundamental herbs of Chinese medicine, and the bark is used for tinctures to treat skin ailments. There's such a powerful connection between trees like larches and healing in China, particularly when it comes to the traditional practice of Qigong, a system of exercise, breath control, and meditation. "Qi" refers to our life force—the energy that moves through our bodies—and "gong" means practice or work. According to the contemporary Qigong Master Robert Peng, the universe is divided into five elements: fire, water, earth, metal, and wood. Peng writes in his book *The Master Key* that wood is the only element "that actually grows. In fact, the tree rings that make up a piece of wood are a testament to the number of springtimes that tree has seen. It follows that wood, the most productive element, is associated with Spring, the season of new beginnings."

*…Where ancient woods have
no tracks of men
Deep in mountains, sounds
somewhere a bell;
Waterfall voice coming
from steep crags
And sun's color cold on
the larches…*

From "On Going by the Shrine of Stored Incense" by Wang Wei, eighth-century Chinese poet and landscape painter, translated by Arthur R. V. Cooper

LARCH ENERGY

To study Qigong is to study the postures (including "Standing Like a Tree") passed down from master to teacher since the fifth century BCE, when Lao Tzu wrote the *Tao Te Ching* or "The Book of the Way," the primary text of Taoism. We can take a step on that path by following this simple suggestion from Robert Peng: "as you walk in the forest you can become aware of the trees, absorb their energy, and be nourished by the Tree Qi." Apply this to the larch—its vital golden light in autumn, the mystery of the conifer that drops leaves and sprouts new ones, and its power to heal us both physically and spiritually.

Linden

The fragrance of linden, or lime, blossoms, which cover the trees from June through August, is the stuff of sense memories and poetry. Brooklyn herbalist Cheryl Boiko put it like this when I asked her about linden flowers: "I love when I'm out and about in late spring… and suddenly my senses are filled with the most delightful, light, sweet fragrance—it always takes me by surprise. I stop and look around and most often I find myself standing under a fully blooming linden tree with the little creamy-white clusters of flowers looking down at me." She went on to explain how the honey from the linden blossoms is a wonderful heart tonic, reducing blood pressure, cholesterol, and plaque, and can also lift the spirits in times of grief. It soothes coughs, can relieve cold and flu symptoms, and, because it is a mild sedative, it can help to ease tension headaches.

Other names for the linden are "bee tree" and "humming tree," both of which are apt. Lindens are very important plants for beekeepers, producing a distinctive, almost clear honey with a rich flavor that evokes mint and lime. The fabled excellence of the honey of the Hyblaean Mountains in Sicily was a result of the myriad linden trees that once covered its sides and crowned its summit. The Roman poet Horace wrote about linden honey, and for the Victorians, saying something was "as sweet as Hybla's honey" was high praise.

HEALING WITH HONEY

Treat yourself to some linden flower honey as part of your wellness and self-care process. People say that taking a teaspoonful each morning during allergy season can reduce symptoms, and a teaspoon before bed can be calming and promote sleep. See if it works for you.

Linden… nectar is poured forth in such inviting abundance that during the period of bloom the trees resound like enormous beehives, for every bee within flying distance is on hand to fill its little… honey-sac, and even on moonlight nights the trees have been known to breathe forth the hum of industry.

From *The Honey-Makers* by Margaret Warner Morley, biologist (1858–1923)

Yucca

It is said that Mormon pioneers crossing the Mojave Desert in the mid-nineteenth century named the yucca growing there (*Yucca brevifolia*) the Joshua tree because the sword-shaped leaves reminded them of the Old Testament story of Joshua reaching to heaven in prayer and welcoming the settlers to the Promised Land. This story may be apocryphal, but whatever one chooses to call it, this is a distinctive plant that grows at high elevations throughout the southwestern United States, Mexico, and South America.

An extraordinary symbiotic relationship exists between the Joshua tree and the various yucca moths of the family Prodoxidae. The plant's pollen is so heavy and viscous that it cannot be carried by the wind and requires the assistance of the moth, which has evolved for just this purpose. The moths collect pollen from the yucca flowers and transport it to other flowers, pollinating the plants. They also lay their eggs in the yucca flowers, and when they hatch, the larvae feed on the seeds within the newly produced fruit.

The yucca is a prolific healer. According to Web MD, it is used to treat "osteoarthritis, high blood pressure, migraine headaches, inflammation of the intestine (colitis), high cholesterol, stomach disorders, diabetes, poor circulation, and liver and gallbladder disorders." In addition, the Navajo Native Americans made soap from the crushed roots of *Yucca elata* for washing the hair and skin and treating dermatological ailments, which is why one of its nicknames is soap tree.

A feisty plant, the yucca can live on about four inches of rainfall per year, but its adaptive qualities go beyond that. To protect the trunk from the desert sun, some species drop their foliage to create their own mulch, and, because they're fire-adapted, they proliferate after wildfires.

BE HERE NOW

The yucca teaches us about the healing power of tenacity, of seeing things through, and of taking care of things. "Yours until death" is the meaning of yucca in Louise Cortambert's dictionary of floriography, *The Language of Flowers* (1819). Not all healing happens quickly, and not all dreams are realized in an instant. We can't do everything on our own. Using the yucca as an example, pause and take a moment to care for yourself, to have patience with where you are right now.

Camphor

I'm certain I'm not the only person who loves the scent of fabric stored in mothballs and that of Vicks VapoRub, and the memories they evoke of grandmothers and nurturing. I also happen to love moths, which is probably not quite as popular a fascination. Even so, there are places I don't want to find them, such as in the afghan my grandmother crocheted almost a century ago. This is where camphor comes in.

As early as the Middle Ages, traders went in search of camphor in the tree's native Sumatra, Indonesia, China, and Borneo, and a distillation of the bark was used as an antiseptic and a treatment during influenza and cholera epidemics. In the thirteenth century, the Venetian Marco Polo referred to camphor in his journals, while in his *Complete History of Drugs* (1748), the French pharmacist Pierre Pomet wrote, "The Oil is very valuable for the Cure of Fevers, a Piece of Scarlet Cloth has been dipt into it being hung about the neck." There's a revered old camphor tree in Atami, Japan, and it is said that each circumnavigation of the tree will add a year to one's life.

It is with camphor's fragrance, though, that most of us connect. Crushing the leaves releases a pungent, spicy odor. Today, the essential oil is used in aromatherapy, as well as in ointments to relieve congestion and muscle pain, although in the past it was believed to ward off snakes and even evil spirits. The tree's wood and shoots can be put through a distillation process, transforming them into a crystalline white powder that looks like snow and is used in massage creams and astringents.

Sumatran camphor was once called "icicle flakes" and "fragrant dragon brains" by the Chinese. It seems that no matter the poetry of the name or the species, every tree is sacred to someone, and the camphor tree is no exception. In India, it is associated with the god Shiva, and camphor incense is burned in religious ceremonies. For me, the camphor tree is sacred because of the humble mothball, which will always make me think of my grandmother. The faint remnants of camphor in the afghan she crocheted take me back to winter afternoons spent in

WHAT'S NOT FORGOTTEN

Is there something evocative about the lingering fragrance of mothballs in your closet, the smell of fabric that brings back a deep and personal memory for you? Focus on it and reflect how the best memories can be deeply healing, opening the mind to the positive and replacing trauma with hope.

her living room, the Michigan snow falling hard against the windows, and feeling secure inside, hopeful, and loved. As Amanda White wrote in *Psychology Today* in January 2015, "A number of behavioral studies have demonstrated that smells trigger more vivid emotional memories and are better at inducing that feeling of 'being brought back in time' than images."

With the eye of the imagination I saw a very ancient lady crossing the street on the arm of a middle-aged woman, her daughter, perhaps, both so respectably booted and furred that their dressing in the afternoon must be a ritual, and the clothes themselves put away in cupboards with camphor, year after year, throughout the summer months.

From *A Room of One's Own* by
Virginia Woolf, author (1882–1941)

PART IV
SEEDS

Awareness, Transformation, and Spirituality 102

Renewal, Transformation, and Spirituality

Trees are a lesson in transformation—from a pip and a promise to towering and enduring. When soil, sunlight, and water converge with a tiny seed at just the right time and place, a tall tree providing shade, lumber, and fruit is the result. I spend so much time wondering how my maple tree got to my backyard. Did someone plant it on purpose? Or was it just the miracle of the wind and weather?

Samara… the first time I heard the word, I fell in love with it. It's the winged nut, or achene, containing each maple seed; children call them whirligigs or helicopters because they spin as they fall. Thoughts of samaras lead to what it takes to become a tree. I've been trying to grow offspring of my maple tree in pots for years, but haven't had much luck. Propagating trees is harder than you might think, which makes the poignant ratio of the thousands that are released to germinate into a single maple tree, or any kind of tree, even more profound.

What does he plant who plants a tree?
He plants cool shade and tender rain,
And seed and bud of days to be…

From "The Heart of a Tree" by
Henry Cuyler Bunner (1855–1896)

Trees such as the hackberry and olive teach us of hope and peace as they change from seed to tree. Others can be about becoming something new, yet remaining the same, like the kapok with its tiny wafting seeds that turn into giants in the forest, or the ebony, whose hardwood is sought-after for all the things it can become. Trees teach us about tending and attending to, like the baobab that protects, the neem that nurtures, and the dragon trees that need our care now before they're all gone. Sometimes, as the cottonwood teaches us, we just have to be quiet, listen, and perhaps start over, like the elm fighting extinction, the pistachio witnessing time, or the pipal that reminds us we don't need to become more tree… because we already are. We can consider the ways the sakaki can guide us to say a prayer of gratitude for the eternity that the sequoia can teach us to see.

Trees are legendary, steadfast, and healing. They're also the way humans can touch the future. A seed is a promise, a hope, and it's not just the promise that trees make to us, but the promise that we make to trees—for what's a tree without the planting, the tending, and the protection? As the medieval mystic and theologian St. Bernard of Clairvaux wrote, "Believe me, you will find more lessons in the woods than in books. Trees and stones will teach you what you cannot learn from masters."

Olive

There are records of olives being gathered in Palestine more than twenty thousand years ago. It is one of the oldest cultivated trees on Earth and perhaps the most sacred. They are treasured for their oil, but, for me, their profound magic is in their fragrance—their delicate blossoms in spring and the heavy perfume of their fruit at harvest time.

In Morocco, it is said that the name of God is written on the leaves of the olive tree. Legend tells that at the death of Muhammad, most trees went into mourning and shed their leaves as if it were fall, even though it was June. But some trees—the pine, the citron, and the olive—did not. In recounting the legend, James Edward Hanauer in *Folklore of the Holy Land* (1907) explains why they did not follow suit: "the olive, as their elder and spokesman, replied, 'You show your sorrow by external signs, but our grief, who care not for the opinions of others… is no less sincere, though inward. Should you cleave my trunk open, for instance, you will find that at its core it has become black with grief.'"

The olive tree is one of the most frequently mentioned plants in the Bible, and represents peace. In the story of Noah's Ark, a dove is said to have brought an olive branch to Noah to show that God's anger and the deluge were abating. It is believed that this branch was from one of the sixteen Sisters, or Olive Trees, of Noah that still grow in the village of Bechealeh, Lebanon. These sacred olives are said to be more than five thousand years old and possibly the oldest-known trees in the world, even older than the bristlecone pines in California. Think about it—these trees have endured millennia of wars, droughts, and who knows what kind of hardships and yet they still stand and bear fruit, their branches steadfast symbols of peace.

HYMNS OF PEACE

As the psychiatrist Paul R. Fleischman wrote in *Cultivating Inner Peace* (1997), "Befriending trees, preserving them, planting them, meditating in their company, are all expressions of the peace-bound heart. We have protectors and friends whose leaves are already humming hymns of peace." I've always loved the song "Let There Be Peace on Earth, and Let it Begin with Me," written by Jill Jackson Miller and Sy Miller in 1955—the title is simple, yet profound. How can we, like the olive tree, manifest peace from the inside outward, renewing our hope for not just nature, but the world?

In stony places where no grass grows, wild olives sprawl; close-twigged, blue-gray patches in winter, more translucent greenish gold in spring than any aureole.

From *The Land of Little Rain* by Mary Hunter Austin, American writer (1868–1934)

Cottonwood

The cottonwood tree, also known as the Carolina poplar, grows primarily in the southwestern United States in landscapes where few other trees can survive. The tree is sacred to many Native Americans. If you cut a cottonwood branch, you'll find the image of a star at its center, and the Arapaho and Cheyenne tell stories of how the cottonwood is the source of the stars—they hide in the earth until they find a cottonwood root and then work their way slowly to the tree's canopy. When the Spirit of the Night Sky needs more light, she asks the Spirit of the Wind to shake the cottonwood tree. Whenever a branch breaks, a star is released into the heavens. Another legend tells how the cottonwood has a spirit force so strong that its branches can move even when the wind is not blowing.

In the spring, cottonwoods make millions of floating seeds, which are dispersed by the wind, traveling as far as twenty miles away on a single breeze. They also travel in streams and rivers, and within twenty-four hours of reaching soil, the seed will sprout. So determined is the cottonwood to propagate that even a fallen branch will sprout if it lands on soil.

Because of all the spiritual connections to the tree, many have avoided burning the wood, but instead listened to the tree for directions. As the Lakota holy man Nicholas Black Elk wrote: "Perhaps you have noticed that even in the slightest breeze you can hear the voice of the cottonwood tree; this we understand is its prayer to the Great Spirit, for not only men, but all things and all beings pray to Him continually in different ways."

Can a man sit at a desk in a skyscraper in Chicago
and be a harnessmaker in a corn town in Iowa
and feel the tall grass coming up in June
and the ache of the cottonwood trees
singing with the prairie wind?

From "Portrait" by Carl Sandburg, American poet, 1878–1967

LISTENING TO TREES

We may not all be able to sit with a cottonwood but, like Black Elk, we can listen for its voice. Probably my favorite way to contemplate trees is to sit with the windows wide open on windy nights and marvel at the sound of the leaves of my maple rustling in the wind. Trees have voices that impart their star-like wisdom.

Ebony

The ebony tree, native to southern India and Sri Lanka, Africa, and Indonesia, is under threat. Its wood is so dense that it can sink in water, and its texture and dark color have been treasured since the ancient Egyptians decorated funerary objects with it. The wood has since been used for everything from piano keys to clarinets to chess pieces. It is beautiful—the raw black core of the tree looks more like stone than wood—and remains so desirable that it sells by the gram and is a heavily protected species.

Although treasured for centuries, ebony was first exported and then exploited by the Dutch in the seventeenth century. The illegal harvesting continues today, particularly in Madagascar. In *The Wall Street Journal* in 2011, Pete Lowry, ebony and rosewood expert at the Missouri Botanical Garden, was quoted as saying that the Madagascar wood trade was the "equivalent of Africa's blood diamonds." Just as with diamonds, there is a black market for ebony. In Sri Lanka, the sale of protected ebony logs is illegal and carries a stiff prison sentence. Many organizations are protecting and defending the ebony tree, such as the African Blackwood Conservation Project. Ebony is smuggled and faked because it is so valuable—a cubic meter (about the size of a clothes washer and dryer) of the real thing sells for over $17,000.

It is interesting to look at the situation the other way around. What can trees give us if we leave them be? Do they have value when left to grow and just be trees? According to Nathaniel Altman in his book *Sacred Trees* (1994), "It is difficult to place a monetary value on the many vital services that trees provide. However, the California Department of Forestry and Fire Protection calculates that a single tree that lives for fifty years will contribute service worth nearly $200,000 (in 1994 dollars) to the community during its lifetime. This includes providing oxygen ($31,250), recycling water and regulating humidity ($37,000), controlling air pollution ($62,500), producing protein ($2,500), providing shelter for wildlife ($31,250), and controlling land erosion and fertilizing the soil ($31,250)."

LOOK AT THE WOOD

Find a piece of ebony, a piano key, an old chess piece, or an inlaid box, and really look at it. Imagine the tree being chopped down and the fresh black heart of a cut ebony trunk. Imagine the forest, the loggers, the traders, the shippers, the carvers, the store, and all the steps it takes to get a piece of that glorious tree to you. Was it worth it? Think about this and it may transform the way you look at the things made of wood in your life: your table and shelves, boxes and fence posts.

The men of Dedan were thy merchants; many isles were the merchandise of thine hand: they brought thee for a present horns of ivory and ebony.

The King James Bible, Ezekiel, 27:15

Pipal

The tree perhaps most associated with transformation—the pipal, sacred fig, or Bodhi tree—is a member of the fig family, with the botanical name *Ficus religiosa*. Native to Bangladesh, India, Myanmar, Nepal, Pakistan, Sri Lanka, China, and Indochina, it is revered in Hinduism as the abode of the Hindu trinity—Brahma, Shiva, and, especially, Vishnu—but is perhaps best known as the tree holy to Buddhism. It was under a *Ficus religiosa* that the young prince Siddhartha sat and reached enlightenment, becoming the Buddha, or "the one who woke up."

More than 2,500 years later, descendants of that tree still grow near the Mahabodhi temple in Bodh Gaya, India. One of these is especially revered as the Buddha's enlightenment tree. There are many legends about it:

When Prince Siddhartha (who became Buddha) chose an ancient Pippala tree (Ficus religiosa) for his final approach to enlightenment, he was following a time-honored custom. The place had been a powerful tree sanctuary before that, and after, the Bodhi tree, the Tree of Enlightenment, became the symbol of Buddhism in general. During the first centuries of the new religion the Buddha was not depicted as a meditating human but as the transpersonal World Tree because he had overcome his human boundaries and become one with the world spirit.

From "Living with the Spirit of Trees" (2000) by Fred Hageneder, ethnobotanist and author

HOLDING THE FOREST IN YOUR HEART

Begin seeing the forests or woods as a place of worship and community and as part of your life and yourself—not as a separate entity. Instead of thinking of them as places to visit, begin to think of them as something of which you are a part. Foster your own way of being or connecting to trees that you can hold with you even when you're in places where there are none.

that its bark never ages, that the heart-shaped leaves never die and fall, except on the anniversary of Buddha's enlightenment, when the tree spontaneously regenerates. Whether the legends are metaphor or fact, the Bodhi tree is a destination and an inspiration for spiritual seekers from all faiths.

The Buddha's association with trees goes back a long way before this encounter with the pipal tree. It is said that of his 150 incarnations before being born as Siddhartha and becoming the Buddha, over forty of those were as a female tree spirit, or deva.

Buddhist and Hindu shrines throughout the world have sacred trees of varying ages and lineages, some directly related to the Bodhi tree. According to *Mahavamsa, the Great Chronicle of Sri Lanka*, written in the late fifth or early sixth century CE, during the third century BCE the Indian emperor Ashoka sent a cutting from the Buddha's pipal tree as a gift to King Tissa of Sri Lanka. He planted it at what became Anuradhapura, a sacred city. A sacred fig tree still grows there today. Now called Jaya Sri Maha Bodhi, it is said to be the oldest living human-planted tree in the world. Although abandoned for many years, the site and the tree now thrive and are a destination for travelers and seekers.

Dragon Tree

Native to the East Indies, Cape Verde, western Morocco, Sierra Leone, and the Canary Islands, where it is primarily found today, the dragon tree is easily recognized: it looks like an open umbrella. In his *Herball, or, Generall Historie of Plantes*, written in 1597, the botanist John Gerard presents a reason for its name. He wrote that after the tree blossoms, the tree produces "berries of the bignesse of Cherries, of a yellowish colour, round, light, and bitter, covered with a threefold skin, or film, wherein is to be seen, as Monardus and divers others report, the form of a dragon, having a long neck and gaping mouth, the ridge, or back, armed with sharp prickles like the porcupine, with a long taile and foure feet, very easie to be discerned."

Dragon trees (*Dracaena draco*) were revered for centuries by the aborigines of the Canary Islands, who used the sap during mummification. A gigantic tree at La Orotava on the island of Tenerife was used as a temple—a way to worship trees from within trees.

The trees are best known for their deep red resin, which has been valued since ancient times for healing, and it is uncanny how much the resin resembles blood. Unfortunately, the color red plays into the dragon tree's story in another way: it appears on the Red List of Threatened Species. Created by the International Union for Conservation of Nature (IUCN), the list is an inventory of the global conservation status of endangered and vulnerable species. It is not just over-logging, industrialization, and tourism that threaten the dragon tree. The trees are dying out because of drought caused by climate change, with their environment becoming increasingly arid.

Extinction leads to further extinction. The dragon trees on the island of Mauritius in the Indian Ocean are dying out, which may be a consequence of the extinction of the flightless dodo bird, last seen in the seventeenth century. The fruit of the dragon tree was a staple of these birds. In return for nourishment, they helped the dragon tree to proliferate by processing its seeds through their digestive tract. Sadly, the dragon tree may soon go the way of the dodo.

The best time to plant a tree is twenty years ago;
the second best time is now.

Chinese Proverb

Baobab

From Suleiman the Magnificent, who presented gifts of baobab fruit to visiting dignitaries, to Antoine de Saint-Exupéry, who immortalized these giant trees in his classic story *The Little Prince* (1943), people have been under the spell of the baobab. Sometimes called the upside-down tree because the branches look like roots, the baobab grows on the Arabian Peninsula and in northern India, but it is especially prevalent in Africa and the island of Madagascar.

The largest succulent on Earth, the baobab is a resilient, steadfast, and patient tree, storing water in its pithy tissue, not only surviving drought itself, but also providing water for people—one of the many reasons it is called the Tree of Life. The baobab also provides food to stave off famine: its leaves, rich in minerals and protein, are used in stews and soups. Its fruit, known as "monkey bread," is nutritious and high in vitamin C. Perhaps this is why the baobab is called "the Mother" by the Sahel people in sub-Saharan Africa. The tree's fibrous bark is used to make rope, baskets, and even clothing.

A baobab tree also provides a safe haven and meeting place under its branches, while hollowed-out trunks have served as homes, bus stops, pubs, and burial places. Its scope of nurturing goes beyond caring for humans. The baobab houses its own ecosystem, from lemurs, bush babies, fruit bats, moths, and honeybees—who return the favor by pollinating—to the thousands of creatures scurrying in and out of its crevices. It is not just a place for the seen, but for the unseen as well. In some parts of Africa, it is believed that baobab trees possess souls or are inhabited by the spirits of the dead—spirits that will remain only as long as the trees protect the forest.

In northern Ghana, there's a sacred grove called Malshegu. According to lore, when local inhabitants were persecuted by Arab slave traders in the eighteenth century, prayers were made to a local spirit, Kpalevorgu, whose oracle was said to inhabit a boulder beneath a baobab tree. They believe their prayers were answered when they fought and warded off the slave traders. For nearly three centuries, this forest has been preserved and protected from threats such as roads and mines, which is testimony to the community's religious beliefs. It has also allowed a partially closed-canopy forest to develop in what is essentially a savanna, or dry grassland. The community still thanks Kpalevorgu for rainfall, fecundity, and protection. In celebrating the spirit of the tree and protecting this sacred grove, they are providing protection for themselves and their ancestors.

The size and height of the tree determine how heavily the ground will shake when it falls. The cassava tree falls and not even the pests in the forests are aware. The baobab tree falls and the whole forest looks empty! Such is human life!

From *The Great Handbook of Quotes* (2014) by Israelmore Ayivor, Ghanaian author

A CYCLE OF CARE

The people and things we take care of also take care of us. Like the baobab, the nurturer and the nurtured are one. Find something or someone in your life—a pet, a friend, or a beloved tree—that you take care of, and appreciate how the act of caretaking nurtures you.

Sakaki

In Shinto—the traditional religion of Japan that sanctifies nature and ancestors—sakaki trees (*Cleyera japonica*) are especially sacred. An evergreen related to the camellia, it is called an "always thriving tree," or *sakaeru-ki*, because it lives even in the winter, bursting forth each spring with sweet-scented, ivory-white flowers.

The sakaki plays a significant role in the Japanese story of creation. When the sun goddess Amaterasu was dishonored by her brother, the storm god Susanoo, she withdrew into a cave and plunged the universe into darkness. To lure her out, hundreds of other gods brought a five-hundred-branched sakaki tree down from heavenly Mount Kagu. On its upper branches they strung five hundred gems, on its middle branches they hung a long mirror, and on its lowest branches they placed offerings of blue and white fabric. Curious, Amaterasu crept out of her hiding place. While she was distracted by her reflection in the mirror, the gods blocked her return to the cave and she stayed above ground, restoring light to heaven and the Earth. This is why mirrors are still hung in the sakaki trees planted near Shinto shrines.

There are more Shinto traditions of hanging offerings on trees and at shrines to connect with the *kami*—deities or metaphors for the spiritual and extraordinary. One involves crafting offering wands called *tamagushi*. This is done by attaching zigzag strips of cloth or paper (*shide*) to a stick, often one from a sakaki tree. The *tamagushi* are then hung from hemp ropes or planted in the ground to purify and bless sacred spaces and remove negative energy.

Another way to use the sakaki as a vehicle for prayers is by making *nobori*. These Japanese prayer flags, or banners—such as the ones representing carp—are a familiar sight and can be large and elaborate or simple streamers made of scraps of fabric or paper. Sprigs of sakaki leaves are often attached to the tops of *nobori*. Each one represents a heartfelt prayer of hope or gratitude. At the great Shinto temples, there are often hundreds of hanging *nobori*, which from a distance can appear as a white cloud around the base of the shrine.

CREATING A NOBORI

In *Glimpses of Unfamiliar Japan*, Lafcadio Hearn wrote: "A pilgrim whose prayer has been heard usually plants a single nobori as a token." Create your own *nobori* or *shide*. Write something meaningful to yourself on a piece of paper and fix it to a tree or by a window that looks out at a special tree. Maybe it is a poem of gratitude, or perhaps a prayer of protection for the trees and the natural world.

At the shrine of
Imperial princesses,
Spring purification rites are performed
As cherry blossoms mingle with
The leaves of the sacred sakaki tree.

"Shrine Blossoms" by Rengetsu, Japanese poet and artist (1791–1875), translated by John Stevens

Elm

The elm is an iconic tree, especially in the Northern Hemisphere. They shade parks and line roads—there are over five thousand Elm Streets in the United States. They're the tree of tire swings and tree houses. They are featured in the writing of hundreds of poets—from Sylvia Plath to Gerard Manley Hopkins, Robert Browning to Anne Bradstreet. The elm is the stuff of folk songs, lyrics, and plays: Titania describes Bottom as an elm in *A Midsummer Night's Dream*, and Irving Berlin and Vincent Bryan sang of the elm in "Woodman, Woodman, Spare that Tree."

Yet, Hugh Johnson, one of my heroes when it comes to tree knowledge, wrote of the elm in a *World of Trees* (2010) as "a tree which almost no one plants any more, and many readers will either never have seen or keep only a distant memory." Originating in Asia more than twenty million years ago, the elm has been decimated over the past century, with most of the adult trees dead. In the 1960s, they were struck by Dutch elm disease, a micro-fungus of the bark, spread by the *Scolytus* beetle. It is called "Dutch" elm disease because it was first identified by Dutch botanists. There are reams of scientific literature about the outbreak and its impact, but for me the decline of the elm is visceral as well. One of my earliest childhood memories is of the systematic felling of the elm trees on our street—a devastating sight. Although there is fossil evidence that this was not the first elm die-off, it was heartbreaking to see elm after elm stricken and then cut down to protect the trees around it.

Isolation has protected some stands of elms such as those in New York City's Central Park, and larger areas of British Columbia and Alberta, and, miraculously, all those in Australia. Scientific innovation is renewing the elm population by developing disease-resistant cultivars. Yet, for many, the elms of song and poetry will exist only in memory or imagination.

PRACTICE EXTINCTION

Imagine an elm tree still alive and vital, its green leaves filtering sunlight, its soaring height, and its sturdy trunk reliable and immovable. Now imagine it gone. We take trees so much for granted as we drive past them in our cars, and chop them down to make room for real estate developments or "improved" views, but if we pause to consider a tree—its biological and spiritual complexity—and then its absence, perhaps we will appreciate it more.

Where mellow haze the hill's sharp outline dims,
Bare elms, like sentinels, watch silently,
The delicate tracery of their slender limbs,
Penciled in purple on the saffron sky.

From "In the Defences" by Elizabeth Akers Allen (1832–1911)

Kapok

The mythologies of most cultures have a world tree that protects the Earth. In Central America, the kapok tree (*Ceiba pentandra*) holds this revered position. There are many legends of the kapok tree as a giant at the center of the Earth, with its roots reaching downward to create the underworld and its branches holding up the heavens, connecting all three realms.

Ancient Mixtecs, Aztecs, and Mayans depicted the spiny-trunked kapok tree on sacred objects such as funerary urns and incense burners. There are accounts of the kapok in the books of Chilam Balam, the handwritten seventeenth- and eighteenth-century Mayan collection of myths, prophecies, medical lore, history, and, it is said, the secrets of the soothsayers. The tree is still revered in Central America today—it alone will often be left standing when all the other trees around it have been harvested. It has been said that it is not uncommon to see a single kapok tree in an open field, a reminder of the forest that was once there.

The seeds of the kapok evoke heaven. When the fruits burst open, they release a cottony material that floats like a cloud and can be blown in the wind for many miles. The tree is native to Mexico, Central America and the Caribbean, northern South America, and tropical West Africa. I love imagining a few fluffy-winged seeds miraculously wafting across the North Atlantic from the Bahamas to Guinea.

KAPOK MEDITATION

The seed fluff of the kapok is gathered and used for mattress batting (wadding) and to fill teddy bears, life preservers, and even meditation cushions. So, sit on a pillow and meditate with the kapok tree. Consider the power and poetry of tiny, almost weightless seeds that can float for thousands of miles, sprout, take root, and become a two-hundred-foot kapok tree anchored in the earth, towering over all the other trees in the rainforests, and reaching to the heavens.

If one plant has a prophetic message for us, it is the kapok tree, the Mayan tree of life.

From *The Forgotten Pollinators* (1997) by Stephen L. Buchmann and Gary Paul Nabhan

Pistachio

TREES AS WITNESSES

Remarkable things can happen under a tree. I have my maple, and I hope you have a tree you love. Go and sit with it and consider all the things that tree has witnessed over the months, years, and perhaps centuries. What occurred beneath, in, or above that tree? How has the world around it changed? (There are bonus points if you eat pistachios while doing so!)

The pistachio, a relatively small tree that can endure harsh desert climates, grows throughout much of the Middle East and countries along the eastern Mediterranean. Its nuts have been treasured for centuries for both their flavor and their nourishing properties—they're an excellent source of protein, minerals, and healthy fats. Not only did Pliny write about pistachios but they were also among the remnants of seven types of 780,000-year-old nuts discovered by archaeologists at Gesher Benot Ya'aqov in Israel.

Legend has it that there were pistachio trees growing in the Hanging Gardens of Babylon, now Hilah, in Iraq, as long ago as 700 BCE, during the reign of King Merodach-Baladan, and mention is made in the Old Testament of the healing balm of Gilead, which is believed to have been pistachio resin. The resin is also an essential element of myron, the holy oil used for chrismation, or sacramental anointing, in the Orthodox Christian Church.

There's an especially meaningful pistachio tree growing in the desert of Jordan. It is said that 1,500 years ago, under this tree—or perhaps its great-grandparent—Islam and Christianity met for the first time. A Christian monk named Bahira saw the tree lower its branches to shade a Muslim boy, Muhammad ibn Abdullah, from the desert sun. Bahira was so moved by his encounter with the child that he identified him as a prophet to his people. In 2007, Prince Ghazi bin Muhammad bin Talal of Jordan prayed beneath this significant tree before initiating "A Common Word Between Us and You," an open letter in which he called for Muslim and Christian leaders to unite and work together for peace and justice and their shared belief in loving God and their neighbor. This led to the formation in 2010 of World Interfaith Harmony Week, which was launched at the United Nations General Assembly to reaffirm that mutual understanding and interreligious dialogue constitute important dimensions of a culture of peace.

In addition to the palm, Syria has several trees that are peculiar to itself. Among the nut-trees there is the pistacia, well known among us. It is said that, taken either in food or drink, the kernel of this nut is a specific against the bite of serpents.

From *Natural History* by Pliny the Elder, Roman author, naturalist, and philosopher (23–79 CE)

Neem

Also called Indian lilac, the neem tree has delicate white flowers, fragrant like jasmine. It is considered a blessed tree because of its many healing properties. It is a digestive aid, antifungal, antibacterial, and antiviral. It has been used in the treatment of diabetes and smallpox and as a contraceptive and sedative. It is also a natural pest deterrent—I once used neem oil to stop a mite infestation in a coffee plant I loved that my son had grown from a bean. It is no wonder that neem trees are traditionally planted near homes in India to ensure good health.

In the north Indian city of Benaras, on the bank of the sacred River Ganges, neem trees form the centerpiece at shrines and in holy places. As David L. Haberman writes in *People Trees* (2013), worshipers adorn the trees with brightly colored fabric, garlands of flowers, and silver or brass face masks, and make offerings of spices, incense, and sweets. Often referred to as "the goddess tree," the neem is revered as a tree of the deity Mahadevi, Mother of Life.

Some goddesses are the stuff of myths and shrines and others walk among us. About 700 miles west of Benares, according to *The Hindu* newspaper (April 2013), the village of Piplantri "in southern Rajasthan's Rajsamand district is quietly honoring and protecting women, practicing its own, homegrown brand of Eco-feminism, and achieving spectacular results." In a culture where females aren't always as valued as males, the residents of Piplantri plant 111 trees every time a baby girl is born, to counter gender discrimination. (I have looked and looked and can find no explanation for why it's 111, yet all the sources are very exact about this number.) Often these trees are neem trees. The village's former *sarpanch* (village head) Shyam Sundar Paliwal initiated this practice in memory of his daughter. He explained, "We make these parents sign an affidavit promising that they will not marry her [their daughter] off before the legal age, [and will] send her to school regularly and take care of the trees planted in her name." If they honor this affidavit, they receive a payment of 30,000 rupees ($480) when the young woman turns eighteen. It's a lovely way to honor and safeguard both girls and trees.

THE MATTER AT HAND

The Hindu scriptures known as *Devi Mahatmya* say, "Though she is eternal, the goddess becomes manifest over and over again to protect the world." How can we plant the neem tree, the goddess tree, either figuratively or literally in our lives? Who or what needs protection and nurturing? Now is the time to take care of the matter. No gesture is too grand or too small. It can be as simple as tending one seed or 111 of them.

The neem tree is the Goddess. It is her body.
The face on her makes it easier for us to connect with her.

A neem tree worshiper in Benares, India, quoted in *People Trees* (2013)
by David L. Haberman, author

Hackberry

For me, butterflies are like living flying flowers, symbols of hope and creative freedom. Butterflies depend on trees for sustenance, and trees depend on butterflies for pollination. When each part of nature works in synchronization with the next, things just feel right. Take a moment to appreciate the myriad miraculous workings of nature around you, how one piece fits into the other. It is definitely a source of optimism.

Trees can teach us about extinction, grief, and loss, but they can also renew our optimism. The hackberry is just such a tree. Caterpillars love the hackberry, and where there are caterpillars, there are butterflies! For me, hackberry trees are a symbol of hope. According to *The Book of Forest and Thicket* (1992) by John Eastman, "Fossils of snout butterflies have been found in Pleistocene deposits that also held ancient hackberry leaves." In North America, the leaves are a food source for the gray emperor, question mark, snout, and tawny emperor butterflies. There are many subspecies of specifically hackberry butterflies—eastern, Florida, western, and desert, as well as the African, common, and European beak butterflies and the poetically named mourning cloak, scarce tortoiseshell, and great purple emperor.

The hackberry was once thought to be a member of the elm family, but it turns out that it is actually part of the hemp, or cannabis, family. Hackberries grow wild through the temperate regions of southern Europe, North Africa, and North America. Hackberry wood has been used to make charms since biblical times. It is said that when King Solomon was building his legendary temple, he asked God for help, and an angel was told to plant hackberry trees to protect the king from the "evil eye." Hackberry juice, made from the leaves, is one of the ingredients of a lovely Korean tea called *gamro cha*, while, among Native Americans, the Apaches include hackberry wood in their sacred fires during religious ceremonies, during which the hallucinogenic peyote cactus is consumed.

So much comes so thick and fast sometimes, like this June when the 17-year cicadas hatched at the same time as the unleashing of thousands of hackberry butterflies. Walking from the car to the house, I have to close my mouth so a butterfly doesn't zip in and avoid stepping on some of the dead cicadas, strangely enough, fed on by the butterflies.

From "Everyday Magic" (2015) by Caryn Mirriam-Goldberg, American poet

Sequoia

Sequoia, redwoods, moon trees—when I finally made it to California to see these trees, to stand with them, they were even more astounding and grander than I had imagined. It is no wonder that so many have been given their own names, such as William T. Sherman, General Grant, and Stratosphere Giant. Hyperion, the tallest-known living tree on our planet, is a 380-foot coast redwood (*Sequoia sempervirens*) that was discovered by Chris Atkins and Michael Taylor in Redwood National Park in California in 2006. Its near neighbors are Helios (376 feet) and Icarus (371 feet). For a sense of scale, consider that all these trees are taller than the Statue of Liberty and Big Ben, and nearly as tall as the Great Pyramid at Giza.

Another sequoia of note is Luna, in which the activist Julia Butterfly Hill lived for a little over two years—from December 10, 1997, to December 18, 1999—to oppose the clear-cutting of the redwood forests in Humboldt County, California, by lumber companies. She resided on a six-by-six-foot platform, weathering freezing rains and El Niño, defying security teams and angry loggers. And it worked! The Pacific Lumber Company agreed to preserve Luna and all trees within a 200-foot buffer zone, and Hill walked on solid ground for the first time in 738 days.

In his diary, the naturalist John Muir described the sequoias as "antediluvian monuments through which we gaze in contemplation as through windows into the deeps of primeval time." Primeval time, indeed—*Sequoia sempervirens* is the only remaining plant from the forests of the Cretaceous period (more than 65 million years ago), and some living examples are older than 2,000 years—yet these ancient trees look toward the future. The average sequoia produces about two thousand cones per year, and each contains about two hundred seeds—which makes about 400,000 seeds every year. About 40 percent of them have the potential to germinate. Now multiply that by a grove or a forest, and that's a vast number of potential trees and continuous hope.

ENDING IS BEGINNING

Sequoias seem a good tree with which to end this book—almost larger than imagination and longer than memory. So, simply plant a tree. Whether you believe in karma or heaven, or just spring blossoms and autumn breezes, a tree may be the closest you will ever get to eternity.

The Sequoias stand listening,
watching, searching the sky,
looking far off, over the hills,
up and down the coast.

From "The Rain" by Virginia Garland
in *Out West: A Magazine of the Old
Pacific and the New,* 1908

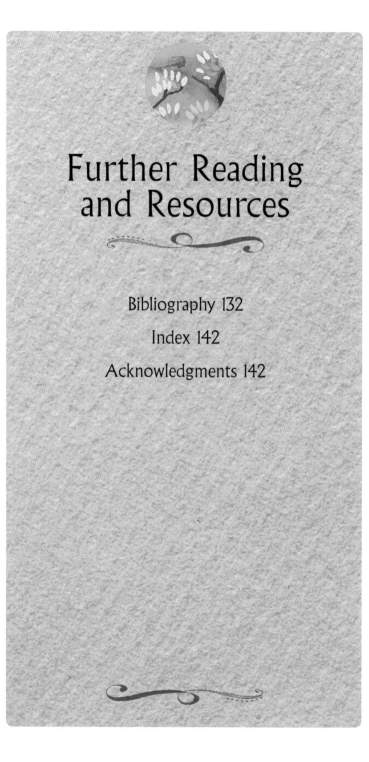

Further Reading and Resources

Bibliography

A

- Abbey, Edward. *Desert Solitaire: A Season in the Wilderness.* New York: McGraw-Hill, 1968.

- *A Common Word* (website). Launched October 10, 2007. Accessed November 15, 2015. www.acommonword.com.

- Albrecht, Glenn, et al. "Solastalgia: the Distress Caused by Environmental Change." *Australasian Psychiatry* 15, Supplement 1 (2007): S95–8. www.ncbi.nlm.nih.gov/pubmed/18027145.

- Alcott, Louisa May. *A Garland for Girls.* Boston: Roberts Brothers: 1888.

- Al-Kuran, Oqba, Lama Al-Mehaisen, Hiba Bawadi, S. Beitawi, and Zouhair Amarin. "The Effect of Late Pregnancy Consumption of Date Fruit on Labour and Delivery." *Journal of Obstetrics and Gynaecology* 31, no. 1 (2011): 29–31. doi.org/10.3109/01443615.2010.522267.

- Allen, Elizabeth Akers. *Poems.* London: Ticknor & Fields, 1866.

- Allen, Elizabeth Akers. "In the Defences." In *Among Flowers and Trees with the Poets: Or, the Plant Kingdom in Verse; a Practical Cyclopaedia for Lovers of Flowers,* compiled by Minnie Curtis Wait and Merton Channing Leonard. Boston: Lee & Shepard, 1901.

- Allingham, William. *The Fairies: A Child's Song.* London: Henry Frowde and Hodder & Stoughton, 1912.

- Altman, Nathaniel. *Sacred Trees.* San Francisco: Sierra Club Books, 1994.

- Anonymous. *The Book of Trees: Descriptive of the Principal Timber Trees, and the Larger Species of Palms.* London: John W. Parker, 1837.

- Anonymous. "Cottonwood Trees and the Stars." Transcribed from the Plains Indians: Cheyenne and Arapaho. *Fort Collins Government* (website). Accessed November 15, 2015. www.fcgov.com/naturalareas/mn-res-pdf/cottonwoods-stars.pdf.

- Anonymous. *The Epic of Gilgamesh.* Assyrian and Babylonian Literature: Selected Translations. Edited by Robert Francis Harper. New York: D. Appleton, 1901.

- Anonymous. *The Language of Flowers.* Translated by Louise Cortambert. London: Saunders and Otley, 1834.

- Anonymous. *Milinda Pañha (The Questions of King Milinda).* Translated by T. W. Rhys Davids. Sacred Books of the East, Volumes 35, 36. Oxford: Clarendon Press, 1890, 1894.

- Anonymous. "Sprig of Acacia." *Short Talk Bulletin* 10, no. 11 (November 1932). www.masonicworld.com/education/files/artoct02/sprig_of_acacia.htm.

- Athanassakis, Apostolos N. *The Homeric Hymns.* Baltimore: Johns Hopkins University Press, 2004.

- Austin, Mary Hunter. *The Land of Little Rain.* Boston and New York: Houghton Mifflin and Company, 1903.

- Ayivor, Israelmore. *The Great Hand Book of Quotes.* N.P.: CreateSpace Independent Publishing Platform, 2014.

B

- **Barash, David P.** "Only Connect." *Aeon* magazine (website). November 5, 2012. www.aeon.co/magazine/science/david-barash-buddhist-ecology.

- **Barker, Diane.** *Tibetan Prayer Flags: Send your Blessings on the Breeze.* London: Connections Book Publishing, 2003.

- **Beilenson, Peter.** *Japanese Haiku.* Mount Vernon, NY: Peter Pauper Press, 1955.

- **Berger, Lawrence.** "Being There: Heidegger on Why our Presence Matters." In *The Stone* (blog). *The New York Times*, March 30, 2015. www.nyti.ms/1G83lwQ.

- **Bernard of Clairvaux.** In Edward Churton, *The Early English Church.* London: James Burns, 1841.

- **Berry, Wendell.** *The Country of Marriage: Poems.* New York: Harcourt Brace Jovanovich, 1973.

- **Berry, Wendell.** *The Mad Farmer Poems.* Berkeley, CA: Counterpoint Press, 2009.

- **Black Elk, Nicholas (Hehaka Sapa).** *The Sacred Pipe: Black Elk's Account of the Seven Rites of the Oglala Sioux.* Recorded and edited by Joseph Epes Brown. Norman, OK: University of Oklahoma Press, 1953.

- **Boleyn, Thomas, and Morteza Honari, eds.** *Health Ecology: Health, Culture, and Human-Environment Interaction.* London: Routledge, 1999.

- **Bradley, T., et al., eds.** *The London Medical and Physical Journal; Containing Correspondence of Eminent Practitioners and the Earliest Information on Subjects Connected with Medicine, Surgery, Chemistry, Pharmacy, Botany, and Natural Science* 37 (January–June 1817). London: J. Souter, 1817.

- **Braudel, Fernand.** *The Perspective of the World.* From *Civilization and Capitalism, 15th–18th Century* 3. Translation by Siân Reynolds. Berkeley, CA: University of California Press, 1992.

- **Browne, William.** *The Works of William Browne. Containing Britannia's Pastorals with Notes and Observations by the Rev. William Thompson.* London: Printed for T. Davies, 1772.

- **Buchmann, Stephen L., and Gary Paul Nabhan.** *The Forgotten Pollinators.* Washington, D.C., and Covelo, California: Island Press, 1997.

- **Buswell, Robert E., Jr., and Donald S. Lopez Jr.** *The Princeton Dictionary of Buddhism.* Princeton, NJ: Princeton University Press, 2014.

C

- **Carpenter, Edward.** *Pagan and Christian Creeds: Their Origin and Meaning.* New York: Harcourt Brace & Company, 1921.

- **Chah, Ajahn.** *A Tree in a Forest: A Collection of Ajahn Chah's Similes.* Compiled and edited by Dhamma Garden Translation Group. Chungli, Taiwan: Yuan Kuang Publishing House, 1994. www.buddhanet.net/pdf_file/tree-forest.pdf.

- **Chalabi, Mona.** "What's the Most Common Street Name in America?" *FiveThirtyEight* (blog), *ESPN*, December 19, 2014. www.fivethirtyeight.com/datalab/whats-the-most-common-street-name-in-america.

- **Clifford, M. Amos.** *A Little Handbook of Shinrin-Yoku.* Santa Rosa, CA: Shinrin-Yoku.org, 2013.

- **Clifton, Lucille.** *Good Woman: Poems and a Memoir, 1969–1980.* Rochester, NY: BOA Editions, 1987.

- **Coleman, Mark.** *Awake in the Wild: Mindfulness in Nature as a Path of Self-Discovery.* Maui, HI: Inner Ocean Publishing, 2006.

- **Collins, Glenn.** "A Tree that Survived a Sculptor's Chisel is Chopped Down." *The New York Times*, March 27, 2008. www.nytimes.com/2008/03/27/nyregion/27tree.html.

- **Cookson, Clive.** "Exhibition of Early Human History at the Natural History Museum," *Financial Times Magazine*, January 31, 2014. www.ft.com/intl/cms/s/2/bedd6a5a-8944-11e3-bb5f-00144feab7de.html.

- **Corbin, Amy.** "Sacred Groves of Ghana." *Sacred Land Film Project* (blog), Earth Island Institute, June 1, 2008. www.sacredland.org/index.html@p=464.html.

- **Crews, Judith.** "Forest and Tree Symbolism in Folklore." *An International Journal of Forestry and Forest Industries* 54, no. 2 (2003), Food and Agriculture Organization of the United Nations. www.fao.org/docrep/005/y9882e/y9882e08.htm.

- **Cushman, Anne.** "The ABCs of Yoga," In *Yoga Journal Guide to Yoga*, a supplement to *Yoga Journal* (1996–7): 2–9, 61–4.

D

- **Dafni, Amots.** "Rituals, Ceremonies and Customs Related to Sacred Trees with a Special Reference to the Middle East." *Journal of Ethnobiology and Ethnomedicine* 3, no. 28 (February 2007). doi.org/10.1186/1746-4269-3-28.

- **Dahmer, Stephen, and Emilie Scott.** "Health Effects of Hawthorn." *American Family Physician* 81, no. 4 (February 2015): 465–8.

- **Darlington, Susan M.** "The Ordination of a Tree: The Buddhist Ecology Movement in Thailand," *Ethnology* 37, no. 1 (Winter 1998): 1–15. www.jstor.org/stable/3773845.

- **Darwin, Charles Robert.** *The Voyage of the Beagle.* New York: P.F. Collier & Son, 1909.

- **Dharmananda, Subhuti.** "Bamboo as Medicine." *Institute for Traditional Medicine Online* (website). February 21, 2013. www.itmonline.org/arts/bamboo.htm.

- **Donovan, Geoffrey H., et al.** "The Relationship Between Trees and Human Health." *American Journal of Preventive Medicine* 44, no. 2 (February 2013): 139–45. dx.doi.org/10.1016/j.amepre.2012.09.066.

- **Drum, Ryan.** "Wildcrafting Medicinal Plants." *Ryan Drum* (blog), updated November 10, 2015. www.ryandrum.com/wildcrafting.htm.

- **Du Toit, Sophia.** "The Baobab—An Ark of Mankind?" *African Aromatics* (website). Accessed November 13, 2015. africanaromatics.com/the-baobab-an-ark-of-mankind.

E

- **Eastman, John Andrew.** *The Book of Forest and Thicket: Trees, Shrubs, and Wildflowers of Eastern North America.* Mechanicsburg, PA: Stackpole Books, 1992.

- **Edgar, Tricia.** "A Weed No More: The Red Alder Has Nitrogen-Fixing Superpowers." *Decoded Science* (blog), May 16, 2011. www.decodedscience.com/a-weed-no-more-the-red-alder-has-nitrogen-fixing-superpowers/549.

Eliade, Mircea. *The Sacred and the Profane: The Nature of Religion*. New York: Harcourt, 1959.

Elliott, Scott. "The Journey of a 9/11 Tree." *The New York Times* video, 6:09. March 10, 2015.

Engebretson, Kath, Marian de Souza, Gloria Durka, and Liam Gearon, eds. *International Handbook of Interreligious Education* (Volume 4, International Handbooks of Religion and Education). Dordrecht, NL: Springer Science+Business Media, 2010.

Environmental Interpretive Center. *Medicinal Tree Tour*. Research by Gregory J. Norwood. Dearborn, MI: University of Michigan-Dearborn, 2003. www.umdearborn.edu/eic/pdfs/webmedicinal.pdf.

F

Farmer-Knowles, Helen. *The Healing Plants Bible: The Definitive Guide to Herbs, Trees and Flowers*. London: Octopus Publishing Group, 2010.

Featherstone, Alan Watson. "Alder (*Alnus glutinosa*)." *Trees for Life* (website). www.treesforlife.org.uk/forest/species-profiles/alder.

Felten, Eric. "Guitar Frets: Environmental Enforcement Leaves Musicians in Fear." *Wall Street Journal*, August 26, 2011. www.wsj.com/articles/SB10001424053111904787404576530520471223268.

Fleischman, Paul R. *Cultivating Inner Peace*. New York: G. P. Putnam's Sons, 1997.

Folkard, Richard. *Plant Lore, Legends, and Lyrics: Embracing the Myths, Traditions, Superstitions, and Folk-Lore of the Plant Kingdom*. London: Sampson Low, Marston, Searle and Rivington, 1884.

Forster, Edward Morgan. *Howards End*. New York: Alfred A. Knopf, 1921.

Frazer, James George. *The Golden Bough: A Study in Magic and Religion*. New York: The Macmillan Company, 1922.

G

Gandhi, Mahatma. *The Essential Writings*. Edited by Judith M. Brown. New York: Oxford University Press, 2008.

Gerard, John. *The Herball, or, Generall Historie of Plantes*. London: John Norton, 1597. www.archive.org/details/mobot31753000817749.

Gibson, Arthur C. "*Eucalyptus erythrocorys*." *Mildred E. Mathias Botanical Garden Newsletter* 5, no. 1 (Winter 2002). www.botgard.ucla.edu/html/MEMBGNewsletter/Volume5number1/Eucalyptuserythrocorys.html.

von Goethe, Johann Wolfgang. "Gingo Biloba" poem (1819), from *West-Eastern Divan in Twelve Books*. Translated by Edward Dowden. London: J. M. Dent, 1914.

Goodall, Jane. *Seeds of Hope: Wisdom and Wonder from the World of Plants*. With Gail Hudson. New York: Grand Central Publishing, 2013.

Gravil, Richard, and Daniel Robinson, eds. *The Oxford Handbook of William Wordsworth*. Oxford: Oxford University Press, 2015. dx.doi.org/10.1093/oxfordhb/9780199662128.001.0001.

H

- **Haberman, David L.** *People Trees: Worship of Trees in Northern India*. New York: Oxford University Press, 2013.

- **Hageneder, Fred.** "Living with the Spirit of Trees." *Mensch & Sein* (blog), Munich, February 2000. www.themeaningoftrees.com/living-spirit-trees.

- **Hageneder, Fred.** *The Meaning of Trees*. San Francisco: Chronicle Books, 2005.

- **Hanauer, J. E.** *Folk-lore of the Holy Land: Moslem, Christian and Jewish*. London: Duckworth & Company, 1907.

- **Hanson, Thor.** *The Triumph of Seeds: How Grains, Nuts, Kernels, Pulses, & Pips Conquered the Plant Kingdom and Shaped Human History*. New York: Basic Books, 2015.

- **Harper, Douglas, ed.** *Online Etymology Dictionary*. Etymonline (website). Accessed October 3, 2015. www.etymonline.com.

- **Haskell, David George.** *The Forest Unseen: A Year's Watch in Nature*. New York: Penguin Books, 2012.

- **Hearn, Lafcadio.** *Glimpses of Unfamiliar Japan*. Leipzig: Bernhard Tauchnitz, 1910.

- **Hébert, Paul D. N., et al.** "Ten Species in One: DNA Barcoding Reveals Cryptic Species in the Semitropical Skipper Butterfly *Astraptes fulgerator*." *Proceedings of the National Academy of Sciences of the United States of America* 101, no. 41 (2004): 14812–17. doi.org/10.1073/pnas.0406166101.

- **Heinrich, Bernd.** *The Trees in my Forest*. New York: HarperCollins, 1997.

- **Hellmuth, Nicholas.** "Sacred Ceiba Tree." *Maya Archaeology* (blog), Asociacion FLAAR Mesoamerica, September 28, 2015. www.maya-archaeology.org/pre-Columbian_Mesoamerican_Mayan_ethnobotany_Mayan_iconography_archaeology_anthropology_research/sacred_ceiba_tree_flowers_kapok_spines_yaxche_incense_burners.php.

- **Hesse, Hermann.** *Wandering: Notes and Sketches*. Translated by James Wright. New York: Farrar, Straus and Giroux, 1972.

- **"History."** *Detroit Tree of Heaven Woodshop* (website). Accessed November 15, 2015. www.treeofheavenwoodshop.com/history.

- **"How a Didgeridoo Is Made—Myth and Facts."** *Didjshop* (website). Accessed November 15, 2015. www.didjshop.com/shop1/HowDidgeridooIsMade-MythAndFacts.html.

- **Hutchens, Alma R.** *A Handbook of Native American Herbs*. Boston, MA: Shambhala Publications, 1992.

I

- **Issa, Kobayashi.** *The Gold Scales: Collected Haiku*. Haiku of Issa (website). Accessed November 16, 2015. oaks.nvg.org/issa.html.

J

- **Johnson, Hugh, et al.** *The World of Trees*. Berkeley, CA: University of California Press, 2010.

- **Jones, Joseph.** *Medical and Surgical Memoirs: Containing Investigations on the Geographical Distribution, Causes, Nature, Relations and Treatment of Various Diseases* 2. New Orleans: Clark and Hofeline, 1876–90.

- **Jung, C. G.** *Abstracts of the Collected Works of C. G. Jung*. Edited by Carrie L. Rothgeb. London: Karnac Books, 1992.

K

• **Kahlil, Gibran.** *Sand and Foam.* Delhi: Rajpal & Sons, 2008.

• **Kaza, Stephanie.** *The Attentive Heart: Conversations with Trees.* Boston, MA: Shambhala Publishing, 1993.

• **Kent, Elizabeth.** *Sylvan Sketches; or, a Companion to the Parks and the Shrubbery: with Illustrations from the Works of the Poets.* London: Whittaker, Treacher, 1831.

• **Kimmerer, Robin Wall.** *Braiding Sweetgrass: Indigenous Wisdom, Scientific Knowledge, and the Teachings of Plants.* Minneapolis, MN: Milkweed Editions, 2013.

• **Kingsbury, Noel.** *Hidden Histories: Trees: The Secret Properties of 150 Species.* Chicago: The University of Chicago Press, 2015.

L

• **Larsson, Maria, et al.** "Olfactory LOVER: Behavioral and Neural Correlates of Autobiographical Odor Memory." *Frontiers in Psychology* 5, no. 312 (2014). doi.org/10.3389/fpsyg.2014.00312.

• **Lee, Juyoung, et al.,** "Influence of Forest Therapy on Cardiovascular Relaxation in Young Adults." *Evidence-Based Complementary and Alternative Medicine* (2014). doi.org/10.1155/2014/834360.

M

• **Macdonald, Helen.** "Dead Forests and Living Memories." *The New York Times,* September 17, 2015, Magazine. www.nytimes.com/2015/09/20/magazine/dead-forests-and-living-memories.html.

• **Mackey, Albert G.** *The Symbolism of Freemasonry: Illustrating and Explaining its Science and Philosophy, its Legends, Myths, and Symbols.* New York: Clark and Maynard, 1869.

• **Main, Douglas.** "What Is Frankincense?" *Live Science* (website). December 24, 2012. www.livescience.com/25670-what-is-frankincense.html.

• **Mann, A. T.** *The Sacred Language of Trees.* New York: Sterling Ethos, 2012.

• **Meehans' Monthly.** *A Magazine of Horticulture, Botany, and Kindred Subjects,* Volumes 4–5 (1894–95). London: Thomas Meehan & Sons, 1894

• **Merton, Thomas.** *New Seeds of Contemplation.* New York: New Directions, 1962.

• **Mesny, William.** *Mesny's Chinese Miscellany: A Text Book of Notes on China and the Chinese in Two Volumes.* Shanghai: China Gazette Office, 1897.

• **McClellan, George Marion.** "Dogwood Blossoms" in *The American Book of Negro Poetry.* Edited by James Weldon Johnson. New York: Harcourt, Brace and Company, 1922.

- **Mirriam-Goldberg, Caryn.** "An Abundance of Cicadas, Hackberry Butterflies, and Rain: Everyday Magic, Day 853." *Caryn Mirriam Goldberg* (blog), June 15, 2015. www.carynmirriamgoldberg.com/2015/06/15/an-abundance-of-cicadas-hackberry-butterflies-and-rain-everyday-magic-day-853.

- **Moir, David Macbeth** in Elizabeth Kent's *Sylvan Sketches; or, a Companion to the Park and the Shrubbery*. London: Whittaker, Treacher & Co., 1831.

- **Morley, Margaret Warner.** *The Honey-Makers.* Chicago: A. C. McClurg and Company, 1899.

- **Morrow, Avery.** "Tree Ordination as Invented Tradition." *AsiaNetworkExchange* 19, no. 1 (January 19, 2012): 53–60. www.asianetworkexchange.org/articles/abstract/10.16995/ane.11.

- **Muir, John.** *My First Summer in the Sierra.* Boston: Houghton Mifflin, 1911.

- **Murray, Justine** (Ngai te Rangi/Ngāti Ranginui), producer. "Whakatauki mo 18 o Haratua." *On Te Ahi Kaa.* Radio New Zealand National: May 18, 2014. www.radionz.co.nz/national/programmes/teahikaa/20140518.

N

- **Natural Standard Research Collaboration, ed.** "Ginkgo (Ginkgo biloba)." *Mayo Clinic* (website). Accessed November 15, 2015. www.mayoclinic.org/drugs-supplements/ginkgo/evidence/hrb-20059541.

- **Naville, Edouard, and Howard Carter.** *The Tomb of Hâtshopsîtû*: Volume 2 of Theodore M. Davis' excavations: *Bibân el Molûk*. London: A. Constable and Company, Limited, 1906.

- **Neil, James.** *Rays from the Realms of Nature; or, Parables of Plant Life.* London: Cassell, Petter, Galpin & Co., 1879.

- **Nicholls, Christine.** "'Dreamtime' and 'The Dreaming'— An Introduction." *The Conversation* (website). January 22, 2014. www.theconversation.com/dreamtime-and-the-dreaming-an-introduction-20833.

- **Norn, Svend, et al.** "From Willow Bark to Acetylsalicylic Acid." *Dansk Medicinhistorisk Arbog* 37 (2009): 79–98. PubMed ID: 20509453. www.ncbi.nlm.nih.gov/pubmed/20509453.

- **Nuruddinzangi.** "In the Shade of a Tree." *Beneficialilm* (blog). March 18, 2013. beneficialilm.com/2013/03/18/in-the-shade-of-a-tree.

O

- **O'Neill, John.** *The Night of the Gods: An Inquiry into Cosmic and Cosmogonic Mythology and Symbolism.* London: Bernard Quaritch, 1893.

- **O'Reilley, Mary Rose.** *The Love of Impermanent Things: A Threshold Ecology.* Minneapolis, MN: Milkweed Editions, 2006.

- **O'Shea, Ellen.** "Black Cottonwood and the Balm of Gilead (*Populus balsamifer* ssp. *Trichocarpa*)." *Radical Botany* (website). December 11, 2012. www.radicalbotany.com/2012/12/11/black-cottonwood-and-the-balm-of-gilead-populus-balsamifer-ssp-trichocarpa.

- **Ovid.** *The Metamorphoses.* Translated by Anthony S. Kline. 2000. Accessed November 16, 2015. ovid.lib.virginia.edu/trans/Ovhome.htm.

P

- **Pakenham, Thomas.** *Remarkable Trees of the World.* New York: W. W. Norton, 2003.

- **Pappagallo, Linda.** "The World's Oldest Living Olive Trees Are Lebanese." *Green Prophet* (blog). January 8, 2013. www.greenprophet.com/2013/01/noah-olive-trees-lebanon.

- **Parker, Jeri.** *A Thousand Voices.* Brooklyn, NY and Salt Lake City, UT: Winter Beach Press, 2011.

- **Pattee, Fred Lewis.** "Tree Language." In *Among Flowers and Trees with the Poets: Or, the Plant Kingdom in Verse; a Practical Cyclopaedia for Lovers of Flowers.* Compiled by Minnie Curtis Wait and Merton Channing Leonard, Boston, MA: Lee & Shepard, 1901.

- **Peng, Robert.** *The Master Key: Qigong Secrets for Vitality, Love, and Wisdom.* Boulder, CO: Sounds True Publishing, 2014.

- **Pennacchio, Marcello, et al.** *Uses and Abuses of Plant-Derived Smoke: Its Ethnobotany as Hallucinogen, Perfume, Incense, and Medicine.* New York: Oxford University Press, 2010.

- **Phillips, Lena Anna.** "A Walk in the Woods." *American Scientist* 99, no. 4 (July–August 2011). doi.org/10.1511/2011.91.301.

- **Pliny the Elder.** *The Natural History.* Edited by John Bostock and H.T. Riley. London: Taylor and Francis, 1855.

- **Pohlen, Jerome.** *Oddball Michigan: A Guide to 450 Really Strange Places.* Chicago: Chicago Review Press, 2014.

- **Potter, John, ed.** *The Cambridge Companion to Singing.* Cambridge: Cambridge University Press, 2000.

Q

- **Qing Li.** "Effect of Forest Bathing Trips on Human Immune Function." *Environmental Health and Preventive Medicine* 15, no. 1 (January 2010): 9–17. doi.org/10.1007/s12199-008-0068-3.

R

- **Rengetsu, Otagaki.** *Lotus Moon: The Poetry of the Buddhist Nun Rengetsu.* Companions for the Journey 7. Translated by John Stevens. Buffalo, NY: White Pine Press, 1994.

- **[Robinson, William, ed.].** *The Garden: An Illustrated Weekly Journal of Gardening in All its Branches.* Volume 34. London: 1888.

- **Rokwaho** (Dan Thompson, Wolf Clan/Mohawk). "Thanksgiving Address: Greetings to the Natural World." Translated by John Stokes and Kanawahienton (David Benedict, Turtle Clan/Mohawk), Original inspiration: Tekaronianekon (Jake Swamp, Wolf Clan/Mohawk). *American Indian Responses to Environmental Challenges.* National Museum of the American Indian (website). Accessed November 15, 2015. www.nmai.si.edu/environment/pdf/01_02_Thanksgiving_Address.pdf.

- **Rowthorn, Anne.** *The Wisdom of John Muir: 100+ Selections from the Letters, Journals, and Essays of the Great Naturalist.* Birmingham, AL: Wilderness Press, 2012.

S

- **Sandburg, Carl.** *Smoke and Steel.* New York: Harcourt, Brace & Howe, 1921.

- **Schauffler, Robert Haven.** *Arbor Day: Its History, Observance, Spirit and Significance; with Practical Considerations on Tree-Planting and Conservation, and a Nature Anthology.* New York: Dodd, Mead and Company, 1939.

- **Schimmoeller, Mark.** *Slowspoke: A Unicyclist's Guide to America.* White River Junction, VT: Chelsea Green Publishing, 2013.

- **Schopenhauer, Arthur.** *The World as Will and Representation (The World as Will and Idea).* Translated by R. B. Haldane and J. Kemp. 3 volumes. Digireads, 2012.

- **Seldin, Ronnie Nyogetsu.** "Blowing Meditation." *Shakuhachi* (website). Accessed November 4, 2015. www.shakuhachi.com/K-Seldin-EssayInterview.html.

- **Seldin, Ronnie Nyogetsu.** "Interview: Getting to Absolute Music." Interview with Mary Talbot. *Shakuhachi* (website). Accessed November 4, 2015. www.shakuhachi.com/K-Seldin-EssayInterview.html.

- **Shakespeare, William.** *Macbeth.* In *The Arden Shakespeare.* Edited by Kenneth Muir. London: Methuen, 1962. Accessed online at shakespeare.mit.edu.

- **Shu Ting.** "To the Oak." Translated by Carolyn Kizer, with Y. H. Zhao. *Poetry* (February 1987), page 254. www.poetryfoundation.org/poetrymagazine/browse/149/5#!/20601005.

- **Silverthorne, Elizabeth.** *Legends and Lore of Texas Wildflowers.* College Station, TX: Texas A&M University Press, 1996.

- **Singh, Mahim Pratap.** "A Village that Plants 111 Trees for Every Girl Born in Rajasthan." *The Hindu* (website). Updated April 13, 2013. www.thehindu.com/news/national/other-states/a-village-that-plants-111-trees-for-every-girl-born-in-rajasthan/article4606735.ece.

- **Smith, Betty.** *A Tree Grows in Brooklyn.* New York: Harper & Brothers, 1943.

- **Smithsonian Institution** in collaboration with the Akwesasne Mohawk Nation. *American Indian Responses to Environmental Challenges. National Museum of the American Indian* (website). Accessed November 15, 2015. www.nmai.si.edu/environment/.

- **Stern, David.** "Shamans: Masters of Ecstasy." *National Geographic*, December 2012. ngm.nationalgeographic.com/2012/12/shamans/stern-text.

- **Sturluson, Snorri.** "Gilfaginning." In *The Prose Edda.* Translated by Henry Adams Bellows. New York: American-Scandinavian Foundation, 1929.

- **Styer, Dan.** "The Quotable John Muir." From www.oberlin.edu/physics/dstyer/Muir/QuotableJohnMuir.html. Accessed November 15, 2015.

- **Sudentas, Ruslan.** "Venik and Venik Massage/Platza Techniques." *Russian-Bath* (blog). Accessed November 14, 2015. www.russian-bath.com/venik.

T
- **Taruhito, Kamo.** "Envoys." In *The Manyōshū (One Thousand Poems).* Translated by Nippon Gakujutsu Shinkōkai. In UNESCO Collection of Representative Works, Japanese Series. New York: Columbia University Press, 1965.

- **Thoreau, Henry David.** *Walden; or, Life in the Woods.* Boston, MA: Ticknor and Fields, 1854.

- **Tolkien, J. R. R.** *The Fellowship of the Ring: Being the First Part of The Lord of the Rings.* Boston, MA: Houghton Mifflin, 1965.

- **Tolkien, J. R. R.** *The Two Towers: Being the Second Part of The Lord of the Rings.* Boston, MA: Houghton Mifflin, 1965.

- **Tolstoy, Alexey.** "It Was in Early-Early Spring." In *Introduction to World Literature: An Adventure in Human Experience.* Edited by Rebecca D. Alcantara, Josefina Q. Cabanilla, and Alejandro J. Casambre. Quezon City, PH: Katha Publishing, 2000.

V

- **Vaughn, Bill.** *Hawthorn: The Tree that Has Nourished, Healed, and Inspired Through the Ages.* New Haven, CT: Yale University Press, 2015.

- **Volmink, Jimmy.** "The Willow as a Hottentot (Khoikhoi) Remedy for Rheumatic Fever," *Journal of the Royal Society of Medicine* 101, no. 6 (June 1, 2008): 321–3. doi.org/10.1258/jrsm.2008.081007.

W

- **Wang Wei,** "On Going by the Shrine of Stored Incense." In *The Deep Woods' Business: Uncollected Translations from the Chinese.* Translated by Arthur R. V. Cooper. London: Wellsweep, 1990.

- **War-Torn Societies Project International, Somali Programme.** *Rebuilding Somalia: Issues and Possibilities for Puntland.* London: HAAN Associates, 2001.

- **Watts, D. C.,** *Dictionary of Plant Lore.* Burlington, MA: Elsevier, 2007.

- **Watts, Thomas.** *Woodland Echoes.* Kelso: J. and J. H. Rutherfurd, 1880.

- **White, Amanda.** "Smells Ring Bells: How Smell Triggers Memories and Emotions." *Psychology Today* (website). January 12, 2015. www.psychologytoday.com/blog/brain-babble/201501/smells-ring-bells-how-smell-triggers-memories-and-emotions.

- **White, J. M.** "Music as Intervention: A Notable Endeavor to Improve Patient Outcomes." *Nursing Clinics of North America* 36, no. 1 (March 2001): 83–92. www.ncbi.nlm.nih.gov/pubmed/11342404.

- **Whitman, Walt.** "The Lesson Trees" in *Specimen Days, Prose Works.* Philadelphia: David McKay, 1892.

- **Wickens, Gerald E., in collaboration with Pat Lowe.** *The Baobabs: Pachycauls of Africa, Madagascar and Australia.* Netherlands: Springer, 2008.

- **Williams, Florence.** "Take Two Hours of Pine Forest and Call Me in the Morning." *Outside Magazine* (website). November 28, 2012. www.outsideonline.com/1870381/take-two-hours-pine-forest-and-call-me-morning.

- **Wolf, Kristen.** *The Way: A Novel.* New York: Crown, 2012.

- **Wong, Ming.** *La Médecine Chinoise par les Plantes.* Le Corps a Vivre series. Paris: Éditions Tchou, 1976.

- **Woodward, Catherine L.** "The Ceiba Tree." *Ceiba* (website), Ceiba Foundation for Tropical Conservation. Accessed November 12, 2015. www.ceiba.org/ceiba.htm.

Y

- **Yeats, William Butler.** "Among School Children." In *The Poems of W. B. Yeats: A New Edition.* Edited by Richard J. Finneran. New York: Macmillan, 1933, 1996.

- **Yule, Henry.** *The Book of Ser Marco Polo, the Venetian, Concerning the Kingdoms and Marvels of the East* Volume 2, 3rd edition. London: John Murray, 1903.

Index

Acknowledgments

One spring afternoon, as my maple tree was just coming into leaf, I had a telephone conversation with Kristine Pidkameny. I mentioned how much I loved trees, told her about the Red Hook Tree, and suddenly—at least in tree time—this book was born. You're the heartwood of this book, Kristine! Thank you.

Much gratitude as well to Carmel Edmonds, Helen Ridge, Emily Breen, Rosie Lewis, Cindy Richards, and the thoughtful readers of CICO for turning that conversation into a book. Special appreciation to Melissa Launay for taking my words, being more tree, and creating such remarkable works of art.

A forest of people provided inspiration and help along the way, especially Ruth Mullen, Jeri Parker, Arthur Goldwag, Susan Lee Cohen, Bonnie Myotai Treace, Mark Schimmoeller, Larry Shapiro, Renae Horstman, Elsie Peck, and both William Pecks. I couldn't have written this book without the sanctuary and sustenance I received from the Red Hook branch of Brooklyn Public Library, the original Baked, Chatham Perk, and Jean Maestre's house on Seaview Street.